BRAIN GAMES™

AMAZING PLACES

PICTURE PUZZLES

pil

Publications International, Ltd.

Image Sources: Dreamstime, Fotolia, Index Open, iStock Photo, Jupiter Images Unlimited, Media Bakery, Photodisc, Shutterstock

Contributing Writers: Holli Fort and Laura Pearson

Front cover puzzles: *Colossal Colosseum*, see page 10; *Water Under the Bridge*, see page 29. Back cover puzzle: *Bean There, Done That*, see page 68.

Brain Games is a trademark of Publications International, Ltd.

Louis Weber, CEO
Publications International, Ltd.
7373 North Cicero Avenue
Lincolnwood, Illinois 60712

Permission is never granted for commercial purposes.

ISBN-13: 978-1-4127-9805-1
ISBN-10: 1-4127-9805-1

Manufactured in China.

8 7 6 5 4 3 2 1

Put Your Eagle Eyes to the Test ■ 4

Level 1 ■ 5

Start off easy with puzzles that feature stunning locations with just a few changes.

Level 2 ■ 46

Pick up the pace and hone your observational powers with these exciting photos.

Level 3 ■ 87

Search these amazing scenes carefully as the changes increase and become subtler.

Level 4 ■ 128

Cover the globe as you test your mettle against these more challenging puzzles.

Answers ■ 169

Put Your Eagle Eyes to the Test

Are you ready to test your powers of observation? Not only are the picture puzzles in this book fun and entertaining, but they also challenge your mind. Just look carefully at the pictures on each page to see if you can spot the differences between them. But beware—the puzzles get progressively harder with each level! The number of changes increases, the differences become subtler, the pictures more densely detailed.

These puzzles are taken from amazing places in the United States and around the world. In addition to the challenge of finding the differences in each, every puzzle has a bit of Travel Trivia, a piece of information that tells you more about the location in each photo.

As you move through the book, you'll hone your observational skills. Keep in mind that we've altered each picture in a variety of ways. You might find the letters on a landmark's sign have changed, a cloud has appeared in the sky, or a rock formation has grown larger or smaller. Remember, some puzzles demand that you pay extra attention, as the changes may be found in the smallest details. Not all puzzles feature just two images. Some puzzles involve finding a single change among a grouping of four or six of the same picture. You'll need to look carefully at all the pictures to discover which one is not like the others.

You can check your work with the answer key located at the back of the book. The original picture is presented in black and white, with the changes circled and numbered. Putting your brain to work and focusing your attention are great ways to find fun and enjoyment during your day. You might even find a few ideas for your next vacation spot! So take a deep breath, clear your mind, and get ready to find all the differences in *Amazing Places Picture Puzzles*!

Modified Mansion

One of these antebellum mansions near New Orleans houses some differences.
Look carefully.

Travel Trivia

Oak Alley Plantation, Vacherie, Louisiana: The massive live oak trees that line the path to the Oak Alley Plantation in Louisiana are believed to be nearly 300 years old.

Signs of the Times

Compare these bustling scenes to see if you can flag down the changes.
Hope this puzzle isn't too *taxi*-ing.

Travel Trivia

Times Square, New York City, New York: Times Square, the famous intersection in midtown Manhattan, is the only area with zoning ordinances that require tenants to display electric signs. Lighted signs larger than 400 square feet are called "spectaculars."

Answers on page 169.

Down by the Bay

Look carefully at these lighthouses, and the differences will become illuminated.

Travel Trivia

St. Michaels, Maryland: The Hooper Strait Lighthouse in St. Michaels is called a "screwpile" because it was built on iron piles that were screwed into the muddy bottom of the bay.

Cover Your Tracks

Compare these photographs of Madison County, Iowa, and see if you can uncover some differences.

Travel Trivia

Madison County, Iowa: The Roseman Covered Bridge, built in 1883, appears in Robert James Waller's novel *The Bridges of Madison County,* as well as the film adapation of the book. Madison County once had 19 covered bridges. The six that remain are listed on the National Register of Historic Places.

Answers on page 169.

Colossal Colosseum

Hunt for all the ways we've altered this ancient amphitheater.

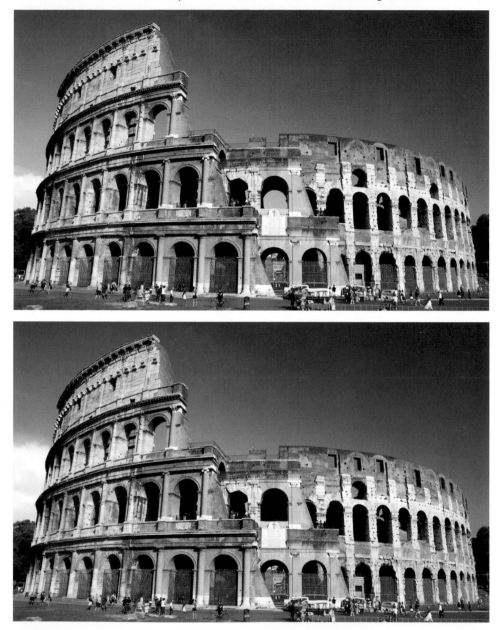

Travel Trivia

The Colosseum, Rome, Italy: The Colosseum was built by the Flavian emperors in the first century A.D. and was designed as an entertainment arena. By law, the Roman ruling class had to organize games—chariot races, staged hunts of wild animals, and gladiatorial battles—to gain public favor.

Answers on page 169.

On the Beaten Path

Be a trailblazing puzzle solver. How fast can you track down the differences?

Travel Trivia

Old Natchez Trace, Tennessee: Originally a 500-mile footpath, the Old Natchez Trace connected Natchez, Mississippi, to Nashville, Tennessee. Although it began as a series of animal trails, it was eventually used by early explorers, military personnel, and post riders.

Cross That (Natural) Bridge

These photos of Natural Bridge State Resort Park are hiding one decidedly unnatural change. Can you find it?

1

2

3

4

5

6

Travel Trivia

Natural Bridge Park, Kentucky: Located in the middle of the Daniel Boone National Forest, the park is home to one of Kentucky's most spectacular sights—a 65-foot-tall, 78-foot-long sandstone arch formed by the Red River. Visitors can also get their toes tapping at the park's Hoedown Island, site of weekly square-dance parties.

Answer on page 170.

Pop Art Puzzle

Become a Master of Fine Art as you critique these photos for differences.

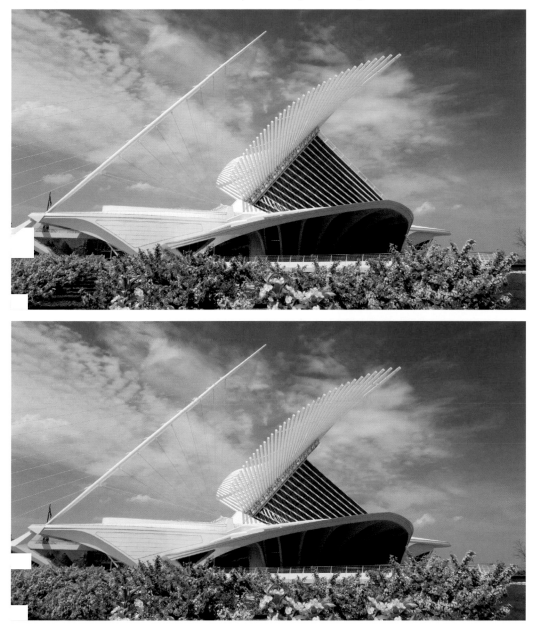

Travel Trivia

Milwaukee Art Museum, Milwaukee, Wisconsin: The museum is made up of three buildings by three different architects. The building shown is the Quadracci Pavilion, a 2001 addition designed by Santiago Calatrava. The "wings" of the pavilion function as a giant set of blinds, protecting the masterpieces inside from harsh sunlight.

In the Shadow of Giants

It may be huge, but don't linger in the shadow of this Giant Sequoia for too long—there are more puzzles to solve ahead.

Travel Trivia

The General Sherman Tree, Visalia, California: While the General Sherman Tree is about 275 feet tall and one of the tallest Giant Sequoias in the world, its circumference is over 100 feet at its base, and its trunk has a volume of 1,487 cubic meters—making it the largest living organism in the world when measured by volume.

Answers on page 170.

A Roaring Good Time

Don't be afraid to put your head between this puzzle's jaws.
There are only a few changes to spot.

Travel Trivia

Art Institute of Chicago, Illinois: Called the Chicago Academy of Fine Arts until its name change in 1882, this museum has been at its present location since 1893. The two lions flanking the entrance were given designations by their sculptor, Edward Kerneys: The south lion "stands in an attitude of defiance," and the north lion is "on the prowl."

A Salty Search

We're *shore* you can spot the single change among these pictures of the Great Salt Lake.

1

2

3

4

5

6

Travel Trivia

Great Salt Lake, Utah: Because the Great Salt Lake is about 12 percent salt, people easily float on its surface. On overcast days, when the sky is the same color as the water, boats appear to float as well...in midair! Not only can visitors enjoy a long salt-water float, but they can also soak up the sun on a beach made of calcium carbonate (lime).

Answer on page 170.

Political Puzzle

Capitalize on your puzzle-solving skills and find all the changes we've made.

Travel Trivia

U.S. Capitol Building, Washington, D.C.: Beneath the U.S. Capitol Building in Washington, D.C., the Congressional subway system connects the Capitol to the House and Senate office buildings. Only staff members and their guests can ride these special subways.

Answers on page 170.

Dammed If You Do

Reach deep into your mental reservoir to find all of the changes between these photos. You shouldn't be fishing for differences for too long.

Travel Trivia

Oahe Dam, South Dakota: Towns, roads, and bridges were relocated beginning in 1948 for the construction of this dam and reservoir. It's the fourth-largest in the United States, stretching 231 miles between Pierre, South Dakota, to Bismarck, North Dakota.

Answers on page 171.

Chimney Rock Riddler

Head out on the trail to find the differences between these photos.

Travel Trivia

Chimney Rock, Nebraska: This formation marked a major landmark for pioneers heading west on the Oregon, Mormon, and California trails. Chimney Rock is featured on the Nebraska U.S. quarter, and it offers visitors the chance to metaphorically pack their wagons for the long journey ahead.

Answers on page 171.

Castle Conundrum

We've altered one of these palatial estates. Finding the differences should be enriching.

Travel Trivia

Hearst Castle, California: The opulent Hearst Castle near San Simeon, California, built by newspaper magnate William Randolph Hearst, boasts 56 bedrooms, 61 bathrooms, 19 sitting rooms, and 41 fireplaces!

Answers on page 171.

Big Bend Backcountry

Feeling adrift? A scenic search through these photos might help you feel moored.
Can you find all the changes?

Travel Trivia

Big Bend National Park, Texas: Not only is the Rio Grande a prominent feature of Big Bend National Park, but this park also offers mountain and desert environments within its 800,000 acres. Visitors can see the sights from the comfort of paved scenic trails or explore the area by foot or float.

Answers on page 171.

Garden Walk

These photos are abloom with possibility! Put your budding skills to the test by cultivating a list of the changes.

Travel Trivia

Biltmore Estate, North Carolina: In addition to touring the gardens (shown) designed by famed landscape architect Frederick Law Olmstead, visitors to Biltmore Estate can see how the other half lived in the opulent 250-room family home that was once the "country retreat" of George and Edith Vanderbilt.

Time to Puzzle
Can you tick off a list of the changes between these photos?

Travel Trivia

Santa Fe, New Mexico: With an average of 300 days a year with sunshine and blue skies, Santa Fe certainly has the market cornered on good weather. This center for Southwestern art is home to a rich cultural tradition influenced by Native Americans, Mexicans, and Spanish and other European settlers.

Answers on page 171.

Land of Lava

Compare these sweeping views of Idaho's Craters of the Moon National Monument
to see if you can find a single change. Don't get stuck!

1

2

3

4

5

6

Travel Trivia

Craters of the Moon, Idaho: In 1969, NASA astronauts Alan Shepherd, Eugene
Cernan, and Edgar Mitchell explored this sea of lava (the result of small fissure eruptions)
while training to go to the moon.

Answer on page 172.

Helping Hand Clasp

We've used our most convincing sleight-of-hand to keep you from solving this puzzle.
Can you find all the changes we've hidden?

Travel Trivia

Tulsa, Oklahoma: *Praying Hands* is a 60-foot-tall bronze sculpture that graces the entrance to Tulsa's Oral Roberts University. Unsurprisingly, this is the largest pair of praying hands in the world. If statues aren't your cup of tea, Tulsa still has plenty to offer, including historic Cherry Street, featuring antiques, galleries, and a large farmer's market.

Answers on page 172.

Search the Alamo

Defend your status as a puzzle champ by rooting out
all of the changes between these pictures.

Travel Trivia

The Alamo, Texas: This mission played an integral role in the Texas Revolution and became a symbol for bravery in the face of insurmountable odds. Today, visitors can tour not only the church, but a library, gift shop, meeting hall, and gardens that all date back to the original mission period.

Answers on page 172.

Water Under the Bridge

Here's a golden opportunity: Find all the differences between these spectacular scenes.

Travel Trivia

Golden Gate Bridge, San Francisco, California: The iconic bridge is not painted gold. The term "Golden Gate" refers to the Golden Gate Strait between the Pacific Ocean and San Francisco Bay. The bridge is painted "International Orange" because the architect Irving Morrow thought it would blend well with the natural surroundings.

Answers on page 172.

Mount Vernon Mystery

This is a puzzle you can really sink your teeth into! Can you find the differences?

Travel Trivia

Mansion House Farm, Virginia: The Washington family home, called "Mansion House Farm" (shown), is the part of Mount Vernon that is open to visitors today. In addition to seeing such fascinating items as George Washington's dentures (made from cow teeth, ivory, and steel), visitors can explore the historically re-created plantation.

Military (Park) Maneuver
Use your best strategy to face the challenge of this puzzle!

Travel Trivia

Gettysburg National Military Park, Pennsylvania: Forty miles of battlefield roads, statues, and memorials mark the area of the Battle of Gettysburg, which is widely believed to have been the turning point of the Civil War. Tours, train rides, golfing, and even ski slopes are among the more modern pleasures to be found in this area.

Answers on page 172.

31

Pioneer Square Search

You'll be courting success if you can find all of the changes between these photos.

Travel Trivia

Pioneer Courthouse, Portland, Oregon: This 1875 courthouse serves as the home of the Ninth Circuit Court of Appeals, making it the oldest extant courthouse in the Pacific Northwest. The graceful historic building is also at the heart of downtown Portland, a city that's bustling with outdoor activities worthy of its pioneer heritage.

Answers on page 173.

An Off Note

Take careful note of these photos, and see if you can find
the single change that's out of tune with the others.

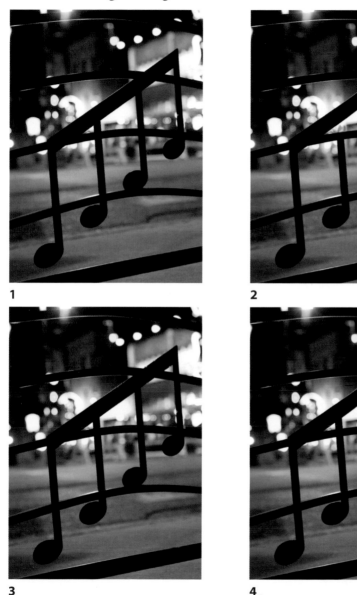

1

2

3

4

Travel Trivia

Beale Street, Memphis, Tennessee: Beale Street in Memphis is known as the "Home of the Blues... Birthplace of Rock 'n' Roll." After decades of neglect and urban decay, this vibrant entertainment district is alive again, with clubs playing live music, restaurants serving Southern food, art galleries, and gift shops.

Answer on page 173.

Old Faithful Finder

We're sure you'll gush with excitement once you get into the flow
of spotting the changes in these photos.

Travel Trivia

Yellowstone National Park, Wyoming: Though Old Faithful is the most famous
geyser in Yellowstone, the park itself contains almost 60 percent of the world's geysers.
In the square mile that contains Old Faithful alone, there are more than 150 geysers.
Yellowstone also features hot springs, waterfalls, and bubbling mudpots.

Answers on page 173.

Eye of the Beholder

Modern art? C'mon…your kid could finish this puzzle!

Travel Trivia

Walker Art Center, Minneapolis, Minnesota: The Walker Art Center is on a
17-acre campus, which includes the Minneapolis Sculpture Garden. The Garden opened
in 1988 and was expanded in 1992 to its current size of 11 acres, with more than
40 permanent installations and several more temporary works on display.

Answers on page 173.

35

The Secret Garden

The changes in this puzzle are few, so there's no reason to get as "lost" here as some previous settlers did.

Travel Trivia

Elizabethan Gardens, North Carolina: The wrought iron gates to the Gatehouse once hung at the French Embassy in Washington, D.C. The Coat of Arms of Queen Elizabeth I of England is over the entrance door, as is a memorial to the 117 English settlers who disappeared in the 16th century as Roanoke's mysterious "Lost Colony."

Answers on page 173.

Presidential Puzzler

It may take a monumental effort to find the single change lurking in one of these photos.

1

2

3

4

5

6

Travel Trivia

McKinley Memorial, Canton, Ohio: This landmark is the resting place of William McKinley, the 25th U.S. president. Visitors can climb the 108 steps of the monument and then take a stroll down a street filled with historical shops at the nearby McKinley Museum. This is also the site of the William McKinley Presidential Library.

Answer on page 173.

Puzzle Mountain Majesties

Finding the changes in this puzzle won't be nearly as hard as scaling
Mt. Mckinley—or tearing your eyes from the moving scenery.

Travel Trivia

Denali National Park, Alaska: It was established as Mount McKinley National Park
in 1917, then known as Mount McKinley National Preserve until 1980. Now at six million
acres, the Denali National Park and Preserve is larger than the state of Massachusetts.

Answers on page 174.

Cape May Cruise

Soak up some ambience as you search these street scenes to spot the differences.

Travel Trivia

Cape May, New Jersey: Unlike the rest of the towns along the Jersey Shore, Cape May is an island and is separated from the mainland by more than just water. Cape May has the look and feel of old-time America, with its colorful Victorian houses and charming shops.

Answers on page 174.

A Puzzle Divided

Can you find the puzzling changes that have taken place between
these pictures of the Lincoln Memorial?

Travel Trivia

Lincoln Memorial, Washington, D.C.: Though this memorial honors our 16th president and excerpts from two of his speeches are inscribed there, the Lincoln Memorial has also been the site of other historic speeches—including the "I Have a Dream" speech of Martin Luther King, Jr., in 1963.

Answers on page 174.

Dunes Day

Don't bury your head in the sand. Take on this challenge
and see if you can dig up the differences!

Travel Trivia

Indiana Dunes National Lakeshore, Indiana: Along the south shore of Lake
Michigan, more than 15,000 acres of dunes comprise the Indiana Dunes National
Lakeshore. The retreat of the last great continental glacier approximately 14,000 years
ago is to thank for the picturesque landscape.

Answers on page 174.

Chichen Itza Chase

Step right up! Can you rise to the challenge of finding all the changes?

Travel Trivia

Chichen Itza, Mexico: Ancient Mayans built this breathtaking pyramid with a special design touch. Visitors to Kukulcan's Pyramid can clap their hands at the base of the steps to hear a distinct chirp. As visitors climb higher and clap, the pitch of the chirps lower. This is believed to be a homage to the quetzal, a native bird prized for its feathers.

Answers on page 174.

A Visual Narrative

Like totem poles, each picture tells a story.
Look carefully at these to spot all of the changes.

Travel Trivia

Saxman Native Totem Park, Alaska: This Alaskan retreat features dozens of totem poles, most of which were reclaimed from abandoned Tlingit villages in the 1930s by the Civilian Conservation Corps and the U.S. Forest Service. The totem poles were collected in Saxman and now form one of the most visually rich and fascinating places to visit.

Answers on page 174.

A Lakeside Property

Can we *wet* your appetite for a good puzzle?

Travel Trivia

Pyramid Lake, Nevada: This stunning oasis in the middle of the Nevada desert covers an area that's 15 miles wide and 11 miles long; the land is part of the Pyramid Lake Paiute Tribal Reservation. In addition to Pyramid Rock, visitors will be amazed by the Stone Mother, a rock formation that looks like a woman sitting on the edge of the water.

Answers on page 175.

Peakaboo

Push your brain to its peak as you search for the changes between pictures.

Travel Trivia

Hallett Peak, Colorado: Hallett Peak is the site of one of the most popular trails in Colorado's Rocky Mountain National Park. The five-mile trek is relatively easy, even for novice hikers, and the views of the surrounding mountains and lakes are worth every bit of the effort.

Launchpad Puzzle

We're sure you'll have a blast (off) discovering all of the changes in these photos.

Travel Trivia

Cape Canaveral, Florida: The ultimate experience for visitors who travel to Cape Canaveral is to watch a space shuttle launch from Kennedy Space Center. Although NASA no longer gives out passes for people to drive their own cars into Kennedy at launch times, tickets are available to join bus trips to watch the launches.

Answers on page 175.

Heavenly Aspirations

Reach for the stars as you search for the single change among these photos.

1

2

3

4

Travel Trivia

The Fountain of Eternal Life, Cleveland, Ohio: Sculptor Marshall Fredericks, a veteran of World War II, created the fountain to honor the 6,000 soldiers from Cleveland who died in the war. Four carved blocks of granite around the figure represent the four corners of the earth, while the figure reaches skyward to rise above the violence of war.

Answer on page 175.

Portland Head Light Caper

Can you find your way to all of the changes in this puzzle,
or will you throw yourself on the rocks of discontent?

Travel Trivia

Cape Elizabeth, Maine: George Washington gave the first order to build the Portland Head Light. Since then, the lighthouse has been rebuilt and repurposed several times. Automated since 1989, the Portland Head Light is now the centerpiece of Fort Williams Park.

St. Paul's Cathedral Chase

Immerse yourself in the spiritual side of life as you
search for changes in this puzzle.

Travel Trivia

St. Paul's Cathedral, London, United Kingdom: Since A.D. 604, a cathedral
dedicated to St. Paul has always stood on the same ground. Today's cathedral was
designed by famed architect Christopher Wren and boasts relics from medieval times,
19th-century mosaics, and an incredible Whispering Gallery.

Flight of Fancy

Let your imagination soar as you search for the changes between these photos.

Travel Trivia

Wright Brothers Memorial, Manteo, North Carolina: Orville and Wilbur Wright chose the sands of the Outer Banks as the location of their first successful flight in 1903. Upon its completion in 1932, the monument became the largest memorial in the United States to honor a living person (Orville Wright was present for the dedication).

Hidden Lake Hunt

It may seem like a mountainous task, but finding all of the changes in this puzzle should actually go swimmingly for you.

Travel Trivia

Glacier National Park, Montana: The lovely valleys of this area were carved by Ice Age glaciers, and the dramatic results can be seen in this International Biosphere Reserve. Hidden Lake (shown here) is one of many alpine lakes formed by glaciers in this area, which the Blackfeet called "the backbone of the world."

 Answers on page 176.

The King's Castle

We would like to "thank you, thank you very much" for trying to find all of the differences between these photos of Graceland.

Travel Trivia

Graceland, Memphis, Tennessee: At 17,552 square feet and with 23 rooms, Graceland Mansion is large but cozy compared to other estates. Visitors can keep busy by visiting the meditation garden, Elvis's car museum, his private jet *Lisa Marie,* and his trophy building, which are all located on the 13-acre grounds.

Answers on page 176.

Volcanic Activity

Get into the flow of things as you search for the single change
among these pictures of Mount St. Helens.

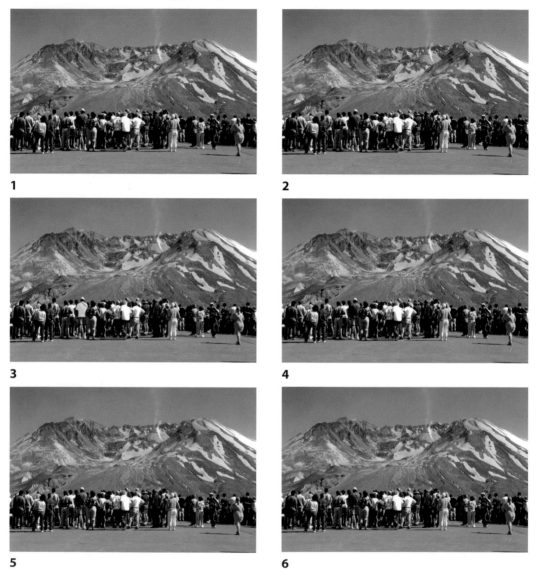

1

2

3

4

5

6

Travel Trivia

Mount St. Helens, Washington: The 230 square miles of forest that were destroyed
during the 1980 eruption of Mount St. Helens are still in the early stages of recovery.
Nature lovers, hikers, and climbers can witness the rebirth of the area while taking in the
panoramic views of the still-active volcano.

Answer on page 176.

Lincoln's Cabin

Create a log of the changes you find in these photos.

Travel Trivia

Abraham Lincoln's Birthplace, Hogdenville, Kentucky: This National Historic Site offers visitors a view of the 16th president's early life. One highlight is the Birthplace Unit, which includes an early 19th century cabin that represents Lincoln's birthplace. The cabin is on display inside the Memorial Building built on the site of the original Lincoln cabin.

Bridge Over Troubled Waters

Tread carefully when looking down for changes.
You'll get a real rush when you solve this puzzle.

Travel Trivia

Multnomah Falls, Oregon: At 620 feet, Multnomah Falls is the second-tallest year-round waterfall in the United States (and the most visited waterfall in Oregon). Though most people visit the falls in the warmer months, adventurous travelers are in for a treat. During extremely cold temperatures, the falls will freeze in a long, solid column of ice.

Answers on page 176.

Red Rock Riddler

Study these pictures closely, and the formation of a list of changes
will come to you!

Travel Trivia

Sedona, Arizona: Sedona's natural beauty and nearly perfect year-round weather
make it a great place for a vacation. Its famous red rock formations, including Coffeepot,
Thunder Mountain, and Cathedral, provide the perfect venue for hiking, riding, camping,
and mountain biking.

Answers on page 177.

Pilgrims' Passage

Shorely you can find the changes between these photos!

Travel Trivia

Plimoth Plantation, Massachusetts: The *Mayflower II* is a reproduction of the original *Mayflower*, the ship that brought the pilgrims to Plymouth Rock. Visitors who explore *Mayflower II* will find themselves in the middle of history, as costumed performers enact shipboard life in the 17th century.

Mayan Mystery

Step by step, unlock the changes made to these photos.

Travel Trivia

Mayan Ruins at Tulum, Mexico: Abandoned by the Mayan sometime in the 17th century, El Castillo, the ancient structure shown here, was part castle, part lighthouse, and part temple. It is believed that many of these buildings were once painted red, white, and blue; red paint can still be seen on the outside of some.

Answers on page 177.

Falls Finder

Ah, the falls in fall! Can you find the single change among these photos?

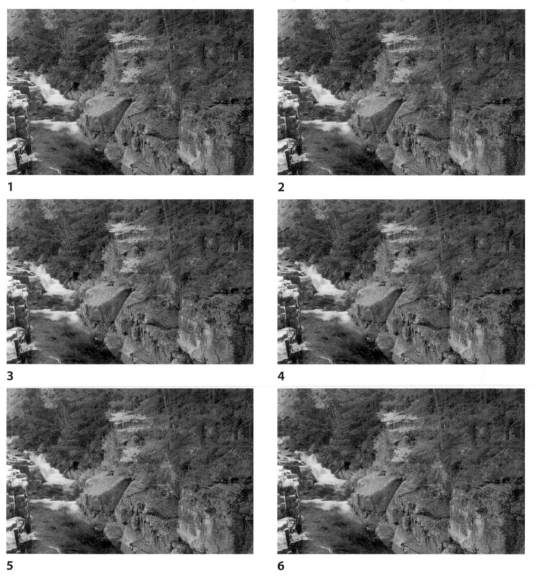

1

2

3

4

5

6

Travel Trivia

Rocky Gorge Falls, New Hampshire: This waterfall is one of New Hampshire's most popular attractions during the warmer months. A short trail leads visitors to the picnic areas around the falls, and a bridge provides a perfect photo opportunity. Though swimming in the gorge is prohibited, it is allowed in the pools above the falls.

Answer on page 177.

Brooklyn Bridge Bungle

Span the gap between these photos by spotting all of the changes.

Travel Trivia

Brooklyn Bridge, New York City, New York: When it was completed in 1883, the Brooklyn Bridge was the longest suspension bridge in the world, and its neo-Gothic towers and intricate framework are still celebrated today. Visitors crossing the 1,595-foot main span of the bridge have excellent New York City views.

Silversword Search

This rare Hawaiian plant faces the threat of extinction...
and so will you if you can't find all of the changes!

Travel Trivia

Haleakala National Park, Hawaii: The silversword cactus (shown) is one of many endangered species that grows in Hawaii's Haleakala National Park. In fact, Haleakala harbors more endangered plant species than any other national park in the United States.

Pueblo Palace Puzzler

If you find yourself out on a cliff looking for the changes in these pictures, don't
dwell on it—just find them all to solve the puzzle.

Travel Trivia

Mesa Verde National Park, Colorado: Mesa Verde National Park in Colorado is the largest cliff dwelling in North America. Visitors will marvel at the simple yet lasting construction materials: wooden beams, sandstone, and mortar. The Pueblo people made this cliff dwelling their home for about 700 years, from roughly A.D. 600 to A.D. 1300.

Answers on page 178.

Bean There, Done That

Reflect closely on these photos to spot all of the differences.

Travel Trivia

Millenium Park, Chicago, Illinois: *Cloud Gate*, a sculpture known unofficially as "The Bean," graces Millennium Park. The polished stainless steel surface of the 66-foot-long, 33-foot-tall work of art offers a reflection of the distinctive city skyline, while at the same time providing a funhouse mirror effect for visitors who stand under its 12-foot arch.

Answers on page 178.

Vineyard Tour

We're sure you'll do a *grape* job spotting all the differences
in these vintage scenes.

Travel Trivia

Napa Valley, California: The vineyards of Napa Valley are legendary for the quality of their grapes. Vineyard tours are available at several well-known sites, and bus tours are available so visitors can take in a variety of wines—with no transportation worries.

Answers on page 178.

Badlands Business

Head out on a search-and-rescue mission for the single change
hidden among these photos.

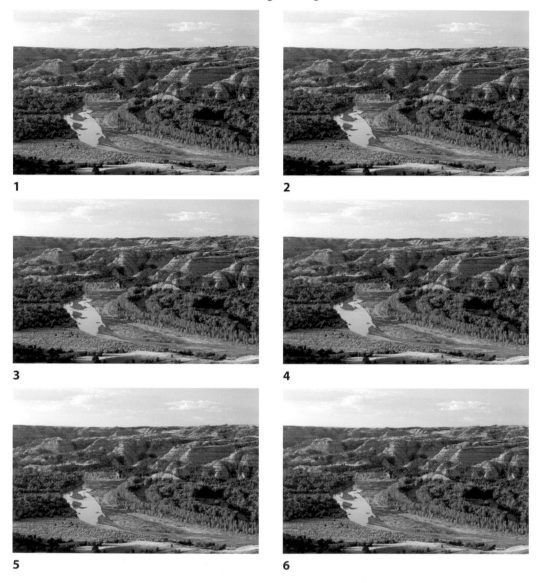

1

2

3

4

5

6

Travel Trivia

Theodore Roosevelt National Park, North Dakota: One of the most stunning
features of this area is the Badlands, a series of layered rock formations that were formed
about 65 million years ago as the planet buckled (a process that is also responsible for the
Rocky Mountains).

Answer on page 178.

Ghost Town Guesser

Earn your spurs by rounding up all of the differences between these two photos.

Travel Trivia

Boot Hill Museum, Kansas: This Dodge City attraction provides a snapshot of life in the 1870s Old West. Dodge City was known as the "Wickedest City in the West," and the abundance of saloons and the paupers' Boot Hill Cemetery are a testament to the town's rough-and-tumble reputation.

Answers on page 178.

San Simeon Search

Delve deeply into these pool pictures as you search for the differences.

Travel Trivia

The Neptune Pool at Hearst Castle, California: Built in the 1920s as the home of newspaper magnate William Randolph Hearst, Hearst Castle sits 1,600 feet above sea level, which often makes it appear to be sitting on top of the fog at its coastal California location. The outdoor Neptune Pool is surrounded by fine art and sculptures.

Answers on page 178.

Waikiki Wander

Take a visual stroll down this ever-changing waterfront to see what's developed.

Travel Trivia

Waikiki Beach, Hawaii: Once the home of Hawaiian royalty, Oahu's Waikiki is a two-mile stretch of incomparable white sand beaches and luxury accommodations. The Waikiki area offers sunbathing, swimming, surfing, diving, and other water sports, along with indoor recreation such as spas and shopping.

A Devil of a Puzzle

Rise to new heights as you challenge yourself
to find the differences between these photos.

Travel Trivia

Devil's Tower, Wyoming: The oldest U.S. National Monument (1906) offers activities to suit every outdoor enthusiast. Hiking, camping, and skiing, and (of course) climbing are popular here. The fastest climb to the top of 1,267-foot Devil's Tower was done in 18 minutes, though it usually takes four to six hours.

Answers on page 179.

Hoodoo Hunt

Map the unique terrain at Bryce Canyon
while you survey the landscape for changes.

Travel Trivia

Bryce Canyon National Park, Utah: Before it was named for Mormon pioneer
Ebenezer Bryce, this park was known as the "Temple of the Gods." Unique rock
formations called hoodoos form spires all over the park, offering an exciting mazelike area
in which to hike. The lack of nearby large cities make it a spectacular place for stargazing.

 Answers on page 179.

Two If by Sea

Keep a lookout for the changes in these pictures
from this advantageous vantage point.

Travel Trivia

Cape Hatteras Lighthouse, North Carolina: Known as the "Big Barber Pole" for
its distinctive stripes, Cape Hatteras Lighthouse is the tallest in the United States. The
original lighthouse was built only on a foundation of heart pine, with no pilings, so the
structure had to be moved inland in 1999 to escape destruction at the hands of the sea.

Answers on page 179.

Historic Renovation

Milwaukee's Pabst Mansion is constantly undergoing renovations.
Can you spot the new crop of changes?

Travel Trivia

Pabst Mansion, Milwaukee, Wisconsin: Visitors to the historic estate can enjoy the 1890s splendor of the home of Captain Frederick Pabst. When Pabst built the mansion, he used all of the latest technology, including central heat, electricity, and modern plumbing. He also added lavish gardens and a glass conservatory.

Answers on page 179.

Set in Stone
There are more changes to find in this level,
so don't take your powers of observation for *granite*.

Travel Trivia

Stone Mountan, Georgia: While the peak of Stone Mountain is 1,686 feet above sea level, the mountain actually extends underground for nine miles at its longest point into neighboring Gwinett County. The summit of the mountain has a view that reaches to downtown Atlanta and, sometimes on very clear days, the Appalachian Mountains.

Answers on page 179.

View Variations

Has the gorgeous view across this river been marred by changes?
Find them all, and then you can decide.

Travel Trivia

Golden Temple of Amritsrar, Amritsar, India: The Harmandir Sahib, or Golden Temple, is the holiest Sikh shrine in the world. In the center of the Golden Temple complex, seemingly floating on the Amrit Sarovar ("Pool of Nectar"), is the Divine Temple, a gold-plated structure that is the most sacred part of the complex.

Grand Canyon Game

Plumb the depths of your observational abilities as you search
for the single change hidden among these pictures.

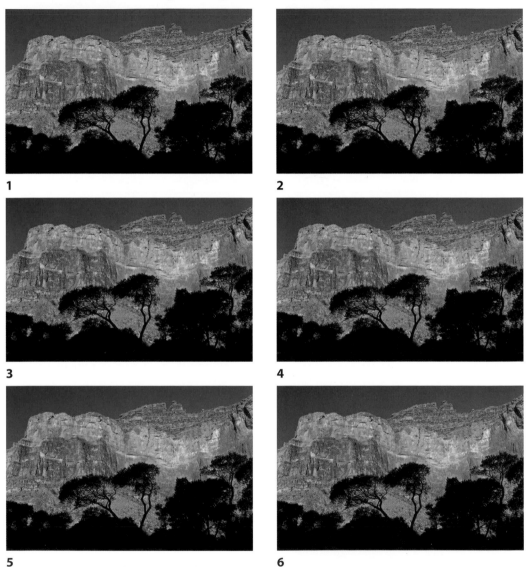

1

2

3

4

5

6

Travel Trivia

Grand Canyon, Arizona: From a distance, the Grand Canyon may look stark and deserted, but visitors will find five of the seven life zones and three of the four desert types of North America contained within its walls. Forests grow at higher elevations, while lower regions are home to a series of desert basins.

Answer on page 180.

Hilton Head Harbor

Look below the surface to find all of the differences in these photos.

Travel Trivia

Hilton Head, South Carolina: Hilton Head Island began developing into a vacation retreat in the 1950s, and it has prospered over the decades. Today, Hilton Head's temperate climate beckons year-round, with championship golf courses, tennis courts, spas, and beaches sitting cheek-to-jowl with the ruins of once-glorious plantation houses.

Beachfront Property

Don't think you can just coast through this puzzle.
Comb through the sand and find those changes.

Travel Trivia

Gulf Shores, Alabama: Gulf Shores is actually one of two seaside towns in the state of Alabama. The Gulf Shores beach is known for its bright, "sugar white" sand; the sand on the beach is made from quartz.

Teton Teaser

Wouldn't it be grand if you found all of the changes between these photos?

Travel Trivia

Grand Teton National Park, Wyoming: The Grand Tetons have their share of beautiful mountain vistas, but visitors may be even more impressed with the spectacular wildlife. Pronghorn antelope, bison, moose, elk, and coyotes roam the land, while bald eagles, great blue herons, and ospreys build nests near the Snake River.

On the Road Again

Don't pack it in—find all of the changes between these pictures.

Travel Trivia

Badlands National Park, South Dakota: Sharply eroded rock formations and one of the country's largest mixed-grass prairies make up this 244,000-acre national park. The area is also one of the richest fossil beds in the world. Ranger-guided expeditions offer the chance to examine both rock formations and fossils on an up-close and personal basis.

Answers on page 180.

Baffling Bridge

Study this landmark London bridge, and see if you come across any changes.

Travel Trivia

Tower Bridge, London, United Kingdom: Towering above the Thames, the Tower Bridge is the world's most famous bascule bridge (a movable bridge with a rising floor that is counterbalanced by weights). In April 1968, a Royal Air Force pilot (quite a show-off) flew a jet fighter between the top span of the bridge and its main deck.

Answers on page 181.

Church Search

Build on your puzzle-solving experience,
and find all the changes we've redesigned into this photo.

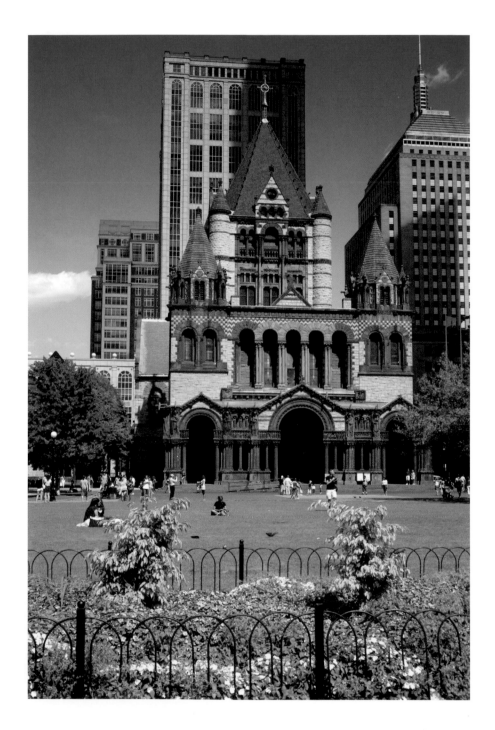

Trinity Church, Boston, Massachusetts: The original site of Trinity Church burned in the Great Boston Fire of 1872. It was rebuilt in Copley Square, and stands as a symbol of Richardsonian Romanesque architecture, with a clay roof, arches, and a large tower.

Museum Mix-up

One of these Venetian-style buildings features some differences.
Hope you have an eye for detail!

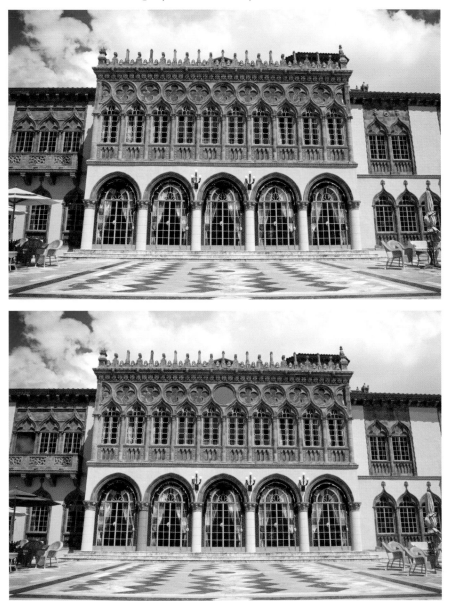

Travel Trivia

John and Mable Ringling Museum of Art, Sarasota, Florida: The Ringling House was established by John Ringling (of the Ringling Brothers Circus) and his wife, Mable. The building is an art museum that showcases Ringling's extensive collection. The Baroque-style Old Master paintings of the 17th century within are among the country's finest.

Answers on page 181.

Storied Estate

Study this distinctive home to see if you can find the distinct differences.

Travel Trivia

Monticello, Virginia: Thomas Jefferson built his home on a hill in Virginia. It reflected many of his architectural innovations. Beds were built into walls and furniture was minimal. He modeled his own bed after ones he saw in France. Tucked into an alcove, it opened on one side to his cabinet and on the other to his dressing room.

Back to Nature

Don't skip rocks—examine them closely (hint, hint).
One of these pristine scenes contains a single change.

1

2

3

4

5

6

Travel Trivia

Acadia National Park, Maine: In the 1880s, Maine's Acadia National Park served as a summer retreat for famous families such as the Vanderbilts, Fords, Astors, Carnegies, and Rockefellers. They altered the natural landscape by building lavish estates. Many of these homes were destroyed in a 1947 fire.

Answer on page 181.

Be on Your Guard

Pay attention, and see if you can find all the ways these photos are not uniform.

Travel Trivia

Buckingham Palace, London, United Kingdom: Soldiers who guard Buckingham Palace are among the most elite of the British Army. The footguards in the Household Division wear red tunics and 18-inch-tall bearskin hats. Animal rights groups have protested the use of bearskins, and the British government may consider alternatives.

Answers on page 181.

Picturesque Park

We hope that searching this awe-inspiring autumn scene
will inspire you to find the differences.

Travel Trivia

Garden of the Gods, Colorado: In the Garden of the Gods, near Colorado Springs, visitors can "read the rocks," which reveal eroded mountain ranges, ancient seas, sandy beaches, and dunes. Snow-covered Pikes Peak can be seen from the park.

Answers on page 182.

Out of the Blue

Examine this illuminated city, and the differences will strike you.

Travel Trivia

Rock and Roll Hall of Fame and Museum, Cleveland, Ohio: The Rock and Roll Hall of Fame was designed by I. M. Pei, a Chinese architect who masterminded the Louvre Pyramid in Paris and the Bank of China Tower in Hong Kong. Before deciding on building in Cleveland, a search committee also considered Memphis, Cincinnati, or New York City.

Parisian Puzzle

Compare pictures of this world-famous tower
to discover all the changes we've made.
Bonne chance! (Good luck!)

Travel Trivia

Eiffel Tower, Paris, France: The Eiffel Tower was built for the 1889 World's Fair. It was designed by Alexandre Gustave Eiffel—who also designed the internal frame for the Statue of Liberty and was nicknamed the "Magician of Iron." The tower was constructed with 18,038 pieces of wrought iron weighing 9,441 tons!

Answers on page 182.

Valley Village

Scan this ancient Pueblo village in New Mexico,
and see if you can unearth some differences.

Travel Trivia

Taos Pueblo, New Mexico: Taos Pueblo is a Native American village that has been inhabited for more than 1,000 years! The ancient, multistoried adobe buildings are home to approximately 150 residents. The buildings also house gift shops where local artisans sell sculptures, paintings, and jewelry.

Answers on page 182.

Lifeguard on Duty

Inspect this colorful lifeguard stand and sandy beach
to see how we've altered the scene.

Travel Trivia

South Beach, Florida: South Beach is known for its unique Art Deco lifeguard stands.
Many of the original stands, designed by architect William Lane, were destroyed during
Hurricane Wilma in 2006, but new vintage-looking stands were built in their place.

Answers on page 182.

Executive Privilege

We've elected you to find all the differences between these presidential estates.

Travel Trivia

White House, Washington, D.C.: The White House has been referred to as the "President's Palace," the "President's House," and the "Executive Mansion," but President Theodore Roosevelt came up with its current name in 1901. Aside from a residence and office, the White House has a tennis court, track, bowling lane, and movie theater.

Answers on page 182.

Go with the Flow

By now, you've tested the waters and should be able to find the single change in this picture puzzle in no time. Just search carefully.

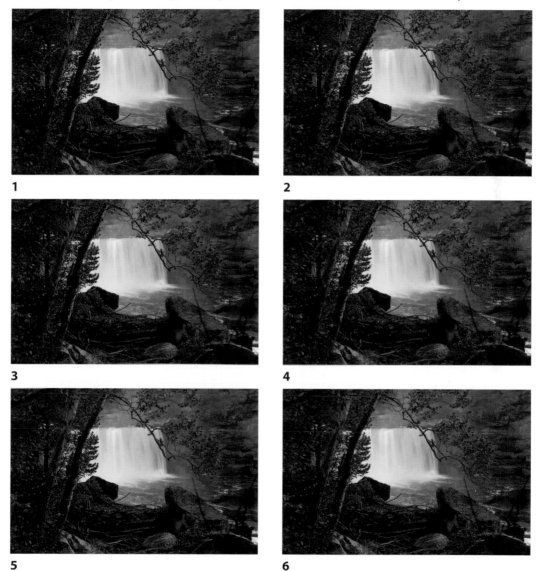

1

2

3

4

5

6

Travel Trivia

Cumberland Falls, Kentucky: Cumberland Falls has many nicknames, including: Little Niagara, Niagara of the South, and the Great Falls. Nearby trails lead to smaller falls, such as Eagle Falls, Angel Falls, and Dog Slaughter Falls.

Answer on page 183.

Life's a Beach

Scan these sunbathers and summer homes.
One of these pictures is swimming with changes.

Travel Trivia

Myrtle Beach, South Carolina: In the late 19th century, Myrtle Beach was a getaway for lumber and railroad workers from Conway, one of the oldest towns in South Carolina. On their weekends off, the workers took flatcars down to the beach. It was many years later that the oceanside city became a major tourist destination.

Answers on page 183.

Beguiling Isle

We've made some changes to this enchanting island in Michigan.
Don't horse around; find them all!

Travel Trivia

Mackinac Island, Michigan: Since the 1920s, no motor vehicles have been allowed on Mackinac Island, a scenic island situated between Michigan's Upper and Lower Peninsulas. Residents and visitors to the island travel via carriage, bicycle, or on foot.

Imperial Estate

The photos of this once-forbidden city house some changes.
Refine your puzzle-solving abilities by investigating these estates.

Travel Trivia

Forbidden City, Beijing, China: *Gugong,* or the Forbidden City, served as the imperial palace in China during the Ming and Qing dynasties. Now called the Palace Museum, this impressive structure is surrounded by a moat and a high wall and contains 9,999 rooms!

Answers on page 183.

Transformed Terrace

One of these pictures of the Bethesda Terrace and Fountain
is overflowing with changes. How many can you find?

Travel Trivia

Bethesda Terrace and Fountain, New York City, New York: The focal point
of the Bethesda Terrace and Fountain in Central Park is the sculpture *Angel of Waters*,
designed by American sculptor Emma Stebbins in 1873. The much-photographed terrace
is the location for many fashion shoots and has been the backdrop for many film scenes.

Answers on page 183.

Mammoth Search

Your puzzle-solving skills are heating up! Compare these pictures
and see how many differences spring to mind.

Travel Trivia

Mammoth Hot Springs, Wyoming: The ever-changing water and mineral deposits in Mammoth Hot Springs (in Yellowstone National Park) create dynamic sculptures. Terraces are formed by water, limestone, heat, and rock, while bacteria and microorganisms add eye-popping colors, including various shades of pink and orange.

Louisiana Landmark

Study these historic State Capitol buildings, and you should spot a single change.

1

2

3

4

5

6

Travel Trivia

Old State Capitol Building, Baton Rouge, Louisiana: The Old State Capitol Building is a significant example of Gothic architecture in the United States. Author Mark Twain, however, was not a fan. In his memoir, *Life on the Mississippi,* he called the building a "little sham castle."

Answer on page 184.

Tropical Paradise

Dive into another challenge! See how this beachfront resort
differs from picture to picture.

Travel Trivia

Cozumel, Mexico: In 1959, when Jacques Cousteau visited Cozumel (an island off the coast of Mexico's Yucatan Pennisula) he discovered that the beautiful coral reefs south of the island (Palancar) were perfect for scuba diving. Scuba diving is now one of the island's most popular tourist activities.

Riverside City

See if you can bridge the gap between these photos of downtown Pittsburgh.
One of them contains some changes.

Travel Trivia

Duquesne Incline, Pittsburgh, Pennsylvania: Pittsburgh has more than 720 bridges. The city is located in Allegheny County, which boasts more than 1,700 bridges! Pittsburgh's three rivers—the Allegheny, the Ohio, and the Monongahela—provide 38 miles of downtown shoreline.

Answers on page 184.

The Birds

This scene isn't something out of a movie thriller,
but use your bird's-eye view to uncover all of the changes.

Travel Trivia

Jama Masjid, India: The Jama Masjid is the largest mosque in India and welcomes crowds of up to 20,000 people during religious services. Non-Muslims can visit the mosque but are not allowed inside during worship times. The mosque is home to many holy relics and an awe-inspiring pulpit carved from a single block of marble.

Answers on page 184.

Wild Wonderland

See the sights! Scan the clouds, bay, and snowcapped peaks
to try to spot the one difference.

1

2

3

4

5

6

Travel Trivia

Glacier Bay National Park, Alaska: Glacier Bay National Park can only be reached by boat or plane. No roads lead to this marine wilderness, and most visitors arrive via large cruise ships.

Changes in Chinatown

We've reconstructed this portion of Los Angeles' Chinatown.
Look carefully and scan the scene for changes.

Travel Trivia

Chinatown, Los Angeles, California: Established in 1938, this is actually the second Chinatown in Los Angeles (the first was an area near Union Station). Visitors can embark upon a self-guided walking tour that includes the farmers market, Phoenix Bakery, Central Plaza, and the Taoist Temple, among many other sites.

Answers on page 184.

Compare the Canals

One of these pictures contains some human-made changes.

Travel Trivia

Venice Beach, California: In 1905, tobacco millionaire Abbot Kinney established Venice, California, or "Venice of America," as a seaside resort town. In order to drain the marshes, he built canals modeled after those in Venice, Italy. When tourists first arrived to Venice, they toured the town on gondolas and a miniature railroad.

Answers on page 185.

Pier Review

Your puzzle-solving abilities are without *pier* if you can find all the changes below.

Travel Trivia

Navy Pier, Chicago, Illinois: The lakefront Ferris wheel shown above is open year-round and offers great views—not only of the Navy Pier campus below, but also of Lake Michigan and the Chicago skyline—during each seven-minute ride.

Answers on page 185.

Hilltop Hunt

This peaceful hilltop hamlet holds a curious number of changes. You'll have to search high and low—but mostly high!—to find them all.

Travel Trivia

Assisi, Italy: Between four to five million visitors make their way to this historic Italian hillside town each year, and the sights are definitely worthwhile. Assisi is best known as the hometown of the Catholic saint Francis of Assisi; holy relics of St. Francis can be found in the town's 13th-century basilica.

Can't See the Forest for the Trees

Fall into a new challenge! See if you can find a single change
in one of the autumnal scenes below.

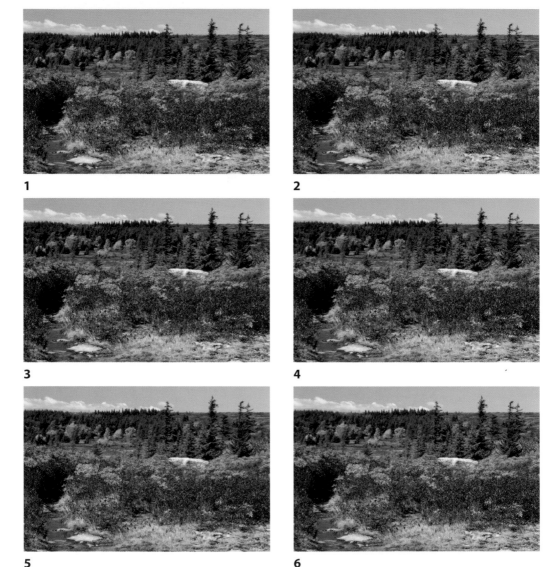

1

2

3

4

5

6

Travel Trivia

Dolly Sods Wilderness, West Virginia: The Dolly Sods Wilderness was once considered an impenetrable forest. In the late 19th century, mills sprang up and the virgin forests were cleared. The Dahle family settled in, burning logged areas to clear grassy areas (or "sods") for grazing. "Dahle Sods" became "Dolly Sods."

Answer on page 185.

Altered Amphitheatre

Study the entrance to the Red Rocks Amphitheatre, and see what changes emerge.

Travel Trivia

Red Rocks Amphitheatre, Colorado: Red Rocks, a geologically formed, open-air amphitheatre in Colorado, is hemmed in by two 300-foot sandstone monoliths, Creation Rock and Ship Rock. Both monoliths are taller than Niagara Falls!

Machu Picchu Quest

Steppe right up to find the single change we've hidden
among these views of the ancient city of Machu Picchu.

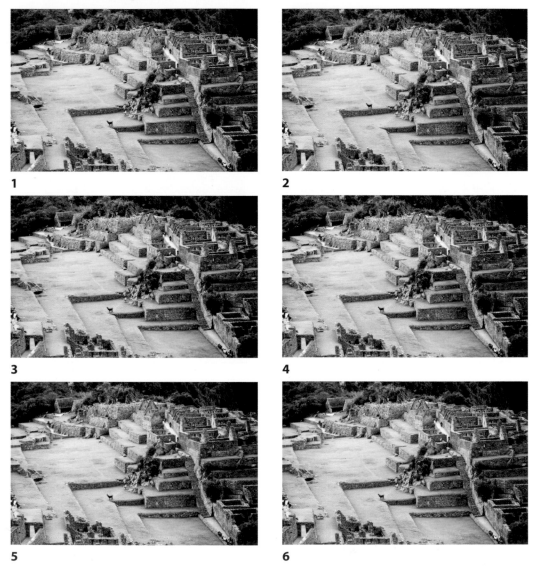

1

2

3

4

5

6

Travel Trivia

Machu Picchu, Peru: Machu Picchu isn't only a site for history buffs—it's also a great
place for animal lovers and birdwatchers. Alpacas (llamalike creatures with soft, warm
wool) roam freely in this protected sanctuary, as do bobcats, spectacled bears, and
vizcachas. More than 420 bird species make their nests in the area.

Answer on page 185.

Water Under the Bridge

Study this landmark bridge in Switzerland. There are changes to uncover.

Travel Trivia

Lucerne, Switzerland: The 14th–century Kapellbrücke (Chapel Bridge, shown) is only one of a multitude of breathtaking sights that await visitors to Lucerne. The scenery is unparalleled, with the mountains rising all around the deep blue water of Lake Lucerne.

Suspend Your Disbelief

We're confident you'll find all the changes to this
suspension bridge and surrounding scene.

Travel Trivia

John A. Roebling Suspension Bridge, Cincinnati, Ohio: The John A. Roebling
Suspension Bridge stretches over the Ohio River and serves as an entry point into
Cincinnati. When it opened to pedestrian traffic in 1866, it was the world's longest
suspension bridge. The Brooklyn Bridge surpassed its length in 1883.

Answers on page 186.

Red Square Search

If you aspire to solve this puzzle, just examine this stunning cathedral for differences.

Travel Trivia

St. Basil's Cathedral, Moscow, Russia: St. Basil's Cathedral, in Red Square, is famous for its bright colors and onion-shape domes. Commissioned by Ivan the Terrible to commemorate his defeat of the Tartar Mongols, it was constructed between 1555 and 1561. The interior of the building contains nine separate chapels.

Downtown Differences

Some changes blew into one of these Windy City scenes. Soak up the view
of these majestic skyscrapers as you try to find them all.

Travel Trivia

Sears Tower, Chicago, Illinois: Soaring to 1,450 feet, the Sears Tower in downtown Chicago is the tallest building in North America and the third tallest building in the world. When calculated to the tip of the building's antennas, the height increases to 1,725 feet!

City Cluster

This crowded city looks like it's constantly under construction.
Can you find all of the changes we've built into these pictures?

Travel Trivia

Venice, Italy: Visitors to the Campanile di San Marco (St. Mark's Belltower) in Venice can take an elevator to the top to get an incredible view of this historic city. The vista provides a unique view of the domes of the Basilica di San Marco as well as the rooftops of the city and the waters of the Golfo di Venezia.

Answers on page 186.

Ellis Island Inspection

We think you can solve this puzzle in a New York minute! Just look carefully.

Travel Trivia

Ellis Island, New York City, New York: Ellis Island served as the country's first federal immigration station. For 62 years, more than 12 million immigrants entered the country though this portal. Originally just over three acres, it grew to over 27 acres due to excess earth from landfills and the construction of the New York City subway system.

Answers on page 186.

Modified Mill

Mull over this mill, and see if you can discover the differences.

Travel Trivia

Mabry Mill, Virginia: One of the most photographed sights in Virginia, the Mabry Mill is a restored sawmill, gristmill, and blacksmith shop on the Blue Ridge Parkway. The National Park Service now runs it as a place where visitors can learn about the milling process and mountain history.

Answers on page 187.

Monumental Challenge

Don't rush this one: Compare the images of this
legendary landmark to find a single change.

1

2

3

4

5

6

Travel Trivia

Mount Rushmore National Memorial, South Dakota: Mount Rushmore receives
approximately two million visitors per year. Originally, the figure of Thomas Jefferson was
to be sculpted on George Washington's right, but after 18 months of carving, the figure
had to be rebuilt on the left. The old figure was blasted off the mountain with dynamite.

Answer on page 187.

Seattle Search

Finding all the differences here is like looking for a needle in a haystack.
(Okay, it's not quite that difficult!)

Travel Trivia

Space Needle, Seattle, Washington: The futuristic-looking Space Needle was built in 1962 for the World's Fair. Standing just over 600 feet tall, it was by far the tallest structure west of the Mississippi when it was erected.

Answers on page 187.

Altered Alcatraz
You can't escape this challenge!
Take a close look, and you'll be sure to unlock the mystery.

Travel Trivia

Alcatraz Island, California: Alcatraz first served as a lighthouse, then a military fortress, then a military prison, and then—most famously—a federal penitentiary for 29 years. The prison held such criminals as Al Capone, Alvin Karpis, James "Whitey" Bulger, and Robert Stroud (known as the Birdman of Alcatraz).

Alley Overhaul

We think this picture puzzle is right up your alley!
Just look carefully as you stroll down this historic byway.

Travel Trivia

Elfreth's Alley, Philadelphia, Pennsylvania: Created in 1702, Elfreth's Alley is only 16 feet wide, a feature typical of the alleys and side streets constructed throughout the city in the 18th and 19th centuries. Having been home to ordinary Philadelphians for more than 300 years, it's one of the oldest continuously inhabited streets in the United States.

Answers on page 187.

Perplexing Parador

These cathedrals were later changed to resorts, so we decided to make some changes of our own. Can you spot the differences?

Travel Trivia

Cathedral of Sigüenza, Spain: The Cathedral of Sigüenza contains two perfectly assembled churches: a Romanesque structure built around 1130 or 1140 and a Gothic-style structure built in the 15th century. Today, the castle at Sigüenza is a parador, or state-run luxury resort.

Answers on page 187.

See Versailles

There are plenty of differences between these picturesque palaces.
How many can you find?

Travel Trivia

Versailles, France: Before the French royal family was forced to relocate to Paris in 1789, they lived in the opulent palace known as Versailles. Thus, it was not just a building but also a symbol of absolute monarchy in France. While the palace is now one of the country's main tourist attractions, Versailles still hosts some political functions.

1 change

Cavernous Challenge

Spelunk the depths of this cave, and see if you can dig up a single change.

1

2

3

4

5

6

Travel Trivia

Carlsbad Caverns National Park, New Mexico: Over 250 million years ago, an inland sea carved more than 300 limestone caves, including Carlsbad Caverns. In 1898, a teenager named Jim White explored the cave, descending 60 feet with a handmade wire ladder. For more than 10 years, he couldn't convince many people that the cave existed!

Answer on page 188.

On the Waterfront

This seaside street scene is crawling with color!
Look carefully to find the changes in these two pictures.

Travel Trivia

Venice, Italy: Venice is well-known for the romance and beauty of its canals. But these waterways aren't just for lovers floating along on gondolas—they also serve as an integral part of the city's public transportation system. Those who visit Venice in the fall and winter should be prepared for high waters.

Classic Architecture Puzzle

Put your powers of observation to the test as you seek out
the changes in these fascinating buildings.

Travel Trivia

Prague, Czech Republic: Prague's Old Town section dates back to the 14th century.
The most-visited historic site in the area is Prague Castle, a 9th-century palace that is
the seat of Czech rulers and the largest ancient castle in the world. By night, Prague has
plenty of nightclubs, operas, theater, and other entertainment.

Answers on page 188.

Boothbay Harbor Hunt

These seaside photos harbor some changes. Can you find them?

Travel Trivia

Boothbay Harbor, Maine: Each April, Boothbay Harbor is home to the Fisherman's Festival, which boasts a wide variety of activities. Adventurous souls will enjoy participating in lobster-crate races, codfish relay races, boat bailing contests, and a bubble-gum blowing competition, with Miss Shrimp Princess presiding over it all.

Answers on page 188.

Full Steam Ahead

By now you've trained to solve more difficult puzzles—like this one!
Search closely.

Travel Trivia

Greenfield Village, Michigan: Greenfield Village and the Henry Ford Museum were designed to show Americans how their ancestors lived and worked in the late 19th and early 20th century. According to legend, Henry Ford set out to buy "one of everything made in America," from canning jars to steam engines, airplanes to rocking chairs.

Answers on page 188.

Harpers Ferry Feat

Go ahead and harp on the differences here. We're sure you'll find them all.

Travel Trivia

Harpers Ferry, West Virginia: This historic town is situated at the confluence of the Shenandoah and Potomac rivers, where West Virginia, Virginia, and Maryland meet. For many people, it is remembered as the town that precipitated the American Civil War due to abolitionist John Brown's raid on the armory in 1859.

Answers on page 189.

Meet Me in St. Louis

We've made alternations around the arch. See how many you can find.

Travel Trivia

St. Louis Arch, Missouri: The St. Louis Arch, known as the Gateway to the West, is an iconic image of the city. It was designed by Finnish architect Eero Saarinen and is 630 feet tall. Since it was built, 11 light aircraft have successfully been flown through the arch.

Answers on page 189.

1 change

Mystery in Mystic

Scan this Mystic Seaport dock to spot the single change we've made to the scene.

1

2

3

4

5

6

Travel Trivia

Mystic Seaport, Connecticut: Founded in 1654, Mystic, Connecticut, gained fame as a shipbuilding center for clipper ships. Today, that heritage is on display at Mystic Seaport's maritime museum and the Mystic Aquarium & Institute for Exploration. It can be found simply by visiting the downtown area as well.

144

Answer on page 189.

New York, New York

Or is it? No, this is the New York New York Hotel & Casino in Las Vegas.
Try your luck at finding all the differences.

Travel Trivia

Las Vegas, Nevada: The New York New York Hotel & Casino in Las Vegas features towers resembling the Empire State Building and the Chrysler Building (among others), a pool resembling the New York Harbor, a half-scale replica of the Statue of Liberty, a roller coaster, and replicas of the Grand Central Terminal and Brooklyn Bridge.

Answers on page 189.

Temple Square Search
Can you tackle this tabernacle puzzle?
Compare the pictures to see what we've changed.

Travel Trivia

Temple Square, Salt Lake City, Utah: The Salt Lake Tabernacle (or, more commonly, Mormon Tabernacle) contains unique architectural features. The Tabernacle roof reflects the bridge-building technique of engineer Henry Grow, and spans 150 feet without relying on center support beams.

Answers on page 189.

Baffling Baltimore

If it floats your boat, compare these scenes of Baltimore's Inner Harbor
and find the differences.

Travel Trivia

Baltimore Inner Harbor, Maryland: The Inner Harbor became a cultural center
of Baltimore in the 1970s. Water taxis transport tourists and residents alike to various
destinations around the harbor, including stores, clubs, and restaurants.

Answers on page 189.

Castle on the Bluff

You'll find several differences between these pictures. We're not bluffing!

Travel Trivia

Fairmont Le Château Frontenac, Canada: Situated atop a bluff, the Fairmont Le Château Frontenac is located in the heart of Old Quebec. Its medieval-style gables and turrets fill the skyline of this 400-year-old walled city, the only fortified city north of Mexico in North America.

10 changes

Hoover Dam Dilemma

We don't want to put a stop to the puzzle-solving fun!
Keep the momentum going.

Travel Trivia

Hoover Dam, Arizona and Nevada: Built in the 1930s, Hoover Dam (located between Arizona and Nevada) was once the world's tallest dam. It was the first single structure to contain more masonry than the famous Great Pyramid of Giza! Now it is part of a system that provides water to 25 million people in the American Southwest.

Answers on page 190.

Ivy League Exam

10 changes

Think you can ace this test? Study the pictures of historic Harvard University, and see if you can identify some differences.

Travel Trivia

Harvard University, Cambridge, Massachusetts: The oldest institution of higher learning in the United States, Harvard was founded only 16 years after the arrival of the Pilgrims at Plymouth. Though never officially affiliated with any religious denomination, the early curriculum reflected the Puritan philosophy of the first colonists.

Answers on page 190.

King of the Castle

We hope this puzzle isn't a royal pain!
Compare these castles—one of them houses some changes.

Travel Trivia

Casa Loma, Toronto, Ontario, Canada: Casa Loma (Spanish for "Hill House")
was the estate of Sir Henry Pellatt, a noted financier, industrialist, and military man.
The mansion is home to lavishly decorated suites, secret passageways, and an 800-foot
underground tunnel.

Answers on page 190.

Building an Empire

We've made some alterations to the Archive building.
Can you catalog the changes?

Travel Trivia

Archivo General de Indias, Seville, Spain: The Archivo General de Indias ("General Archive of the Indies") houses important documents relating to the Spanish Empire in the Americas and the Philippines. The building was commissioned by Philip II in 1572 and designed by architect Juan de Herrera.

Survey the Sandstone...

...and see if you can find the differences. Tread carefully
over this rocky vista, and leave no stone unturned!

Travel Trivia

Arches National Park, Utah: Arches National Park is home to more than 2,000 natural arches, including the Delicate Arch, a world-famous geological formation. It is depicted on Utah license plates, and during the torch relay for the 2002 Winter Olympics in Salt Lake City, a runner passed through the arch.

Answers on page 190.

Something's Fishy

We've made some changes to this charming Norwegian village.
Can you reel 'em in?

Travel Trivia

Lofoten Islands, Norway: As the world's fourth largest oil exporter, Norway is one of the wealthiest countries in the world. It also has rich supplies of forests, hydropower, minerals, and fish. It exports an enormous amount of seafood, often ranking as one of the world's top seafood exporters.

Answers on page 191.

Fountain Frenzy

One of these pictures is overflowing with changes.
Make a splash and find them all!

Travel Trivia

Peterhof, St. Petersburg, Russia: The royal estate of Peterhof is known as the "capital of Russian fountains," or the "Russian Versailles." The impressive Grand Cascade is one of the largest fountain groupings in the world and stretches from the palace to the Baltic Sea.

12 changes

A Graceful Entry

You are cordially invited to find all the changes made to this gorgeous building.

Travel Trivia

Budapest, Hungary: Visitors to Budapest can enjoy several world-class museums, including the Ludwig Museum of Contemporary Art (shown). But Budapest has wonders underground, as well—namely, 118 hot springs and boreholes, which supply the city's abundant spas and baths with naturally heated water.

Answers on page 191.

*Inn*dulge in a Challenge

We've made some changes here. Will you resort to finding them all?

Travel Trivia

Castle Hill Inn, Newport, Rhode Island: Once the summer residence of a Harvard marine biologist, the peaceful Castle Hill Inn now offers visitors the chance to experience Victorian seacoast life. Newport County is home to a variety of mansions, reflecting 250 years of American history.

Building Colors

These buildings may be decorated with three colors,
but there are far more changes in the photos below.

Travel Trivia

Vannes, France: Streets filled with 16th-century colombage (half-timbered) houses line the streets of Vannes. The city's streets may get crowded during peak tourist months, but that only affords the perfect opportunity to take a boat cruise around the islands in the Gulf of Morbihan, which contain Neolithic ruins slowly being reclaimed by the sea.

Panoramic Puzzle

There's a challenge on the horizon! Study this ceramic mosaic in Spain—as well as the surrounding scene—for all the changes we made.

Travel Trivia

Barcelona, Spain: From ancient Roman ruins and medieval districts to Gaudí's Modern masterpiece Casa Batlló and the sporting facilities created for the 1992 Olympic Games, Barcelona offers a wide variety of historical and cultural sites. This view from Parque Güell showcases Barcelona's splendid vistas and its welcoming seaside environment.

Answers on page 191.

11 changes

On the Boardwalk

This puzzle is bustling with changes. Can you find them all?

Travel Trivia

Atlantic City, New Jersey: From the glitz of the casinos and the bustle of the boardwalk to the peace of fishing, boating, and golfing, Atlantic City has it all. The famed Atlantic City Boardwalk offers landmarks Lucy the Elephant and Storybook Land, along with plenty of shopping, dining, gambling, and (of course) saltwater taffy.

Answers on page 192.

Devilish Duty

Compare these pictures of Devil's Hall in Texas,
and see if you can scare up a single change.

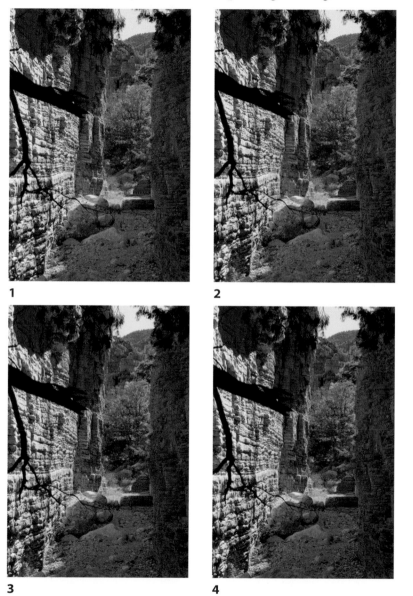

1

2

3

4

Travel Trivia

Guadalupe Mountains National Park, Texas: While featuring hiking trails like Devil's Hall, the only officially designated wilderness in the Guadalupe Mountains contains the world's best example of a fossilized reef. More than 10,000 years of human history are contained within, including battles between Buffalo Soldiers and Mescalero Apaches.

State-of-the-Art Building

Study the Empire State Building and surrounding skyscrapers.
We've constructed some changes.

Travel Trivia

Empire State Building, New York City, New York: The Empire State Building took only one year and 45 days to build. Its height is 1,454 feet from the ground to the top of its lightning rod.

Answers on page 192.

Contend with the Canal

Come ashore to find the changes that are submerged in these pictures.

Travel Trivia

Amsterdam, Netherlands: The dignified historic buildings that line Amsterdam's canals house glimpses into the culture and history of the region, including the FOAM photography museum, Tassenmuseum Hendrikje (Museum of Bags and Purses), Biblical Museum, and Museum Willet-Holthuysen (a preserved 19th-century home).

Wondrous Wall

1 change

You can't really see the Great Wall of China from the moon, but can you spot a single change in this puzzle from right where you're sitting?

1

2

3

4

5

6

Travel Trivia

Great Wall of China: Stretching 4,163 miles, the Great Wall of China is indeed great! It was constructed approximately 2,000 years ago, and the Wall shows definite signs of age. In fact, some sections have fallen into ruin due to erosion from sandstorms.

Answer on page 192.

Riverside Secrets

It's no secret that this puzzle is tricky!
Can you decode these pictures to find all the changes?

Travel Trivia

Varanasi, India: Varanasi is one of India's holy cities, with numerous temples and places of worship. Pilgrims can marvel at the incomparable (and supposedly termite-free) woodwork of Nepali Temple, the layered spires of the 8th-century Durga Temple, and the gold plating of the intricate Kashi Vishwanath Temple and Gyanvapi Mosque.

Answers on page 192.

LEVEL 1

■ Modified Mansion, *(page 5)* **1.** Gap in trees filled in; **2.** grass covered patch of dirt; **3.** door turned black; **4.** shadows deleted; **5.** leaves added.

■ Signs of the Times, *(page 6)* **1.** Arrow and crossbar erased; **2.** person appeared; **3.** N.Y.C. TAXI moved down; **4.** sign got longer; **5.** OFF DUTY erased.

■ Down by the Bay, *(page 7)* **1.** Grass appeared; **2.** part of roof turned gray; **3.** round top deleted; **4.** drain pipe moved right; **5.** trash can appeared.

■ Cover Your Tracks, *(pages 8–9)* **1.** Cloud got bigger; **2.** tree appeared; **3.** treetop pruned; **4.** petals grew.

■ Colossal Colosseum, *(page 10)* **1.** Cloud raised; **2.** person moved right; **3.** archway darkened; **4.** window added; **5.** archway filled in.

■ On the Beaten Path, *(page 11)* **1.** Tree grew; **2.** leaves added; **3.** branch appeared; **4.** branch broke off; **5.** sun setting—shadows appeared.

Cross That (Natural) Bridge, *(page 12)*
1. Orange leaves turned green in picture 3.

Pop Art Puzzle, *(page 13)* **1.** Cloud drifted
away; **2.** bushes grew over stairs; **3.** building segment
removed; **4.** flowers added.

In the Shadow of Giants, *(page 14)* **1.** Leaves
blocked the sky; **2.** post removed; **3.** A changed to E;
4. another bolt added.

A Roaring Good Time, *(page 15)* **1.** Column
of windows installed; **2.** street lights removed; **3.** lion
shaved its goatee; **4.** pole taken down—how does the
flag still fly?

A Salty Search, *(page 16)* **1.** Rock added in
picture 1.

Political Puzzle, *(page 17)* **1.** Tree bigger;
2. row of windows filled in; **3.** man on bicycle changed
direction; **4.** people moved on; **5.** wall extended right.

■ **Dammed If You Do,** *(page 18–19)* **1.** Stack added; **2.** tank missing; **3.** person moved left; **4.** stripes removed from stack.

■ **Big Bend Backcountry,** *(page 22)* **1.** Paddle head missing—up the creek?; **2.** life jacket now pink; **3.** hat turned black; **4.** oar longer; **5.** trees grew on rocks.

■ **Chimney Rock Riddler,** *(page 20)* **1.** Grass removed; **2.** cloud added; **3.** more buildings appeared; **4.** another chimney added (and we thought that rock was unique).

■ **Garden Walk,** *(page 23)* **1.** Yellow pansies turned red; **2.** cloud disappeared; **3.** tree grew; **4.** opening bricked over.

■ **Castle Conundrum,** *(page 21)* **1.** Palm tree taller; **2.** pink flower appeared; **3.** archway opening turned black; **4.** leaf got bigger; **5.** window filled in.

■ **Time to Puzzle,** *(page 24)* **1.** Chimney taller; **2.** doorway missing; **3.** post removed; **4.** circle became square; **5.** dark pink line erased.

Land of Lava, *(page 25)* **1.** Tree sprouted in picture 6.

■ **Water Under the Bridge,** *(page 29)* **1.** Flag moved right; **2.** base got bigger; **3.** horizontal bar deleted; **4.** trees added.

■ **Helping Hand Clasp,** *(pages 26–27)* **1.** Pole taller; **2.** UNIVERSITY became UNIVERCITE; **3.** tree grew; **4.** bush added.

■ **Mount Vernon Mystery,** *(page 30)* **1.** Part of roof removed; **2.** black shirt became green; **3.** oval window became rectangular; **4.** sundial removed; **5.** chimney taller.

■ **Search the Alamo,** *(page 28)* **1.** Star added (now it's the "Not-So-Lone Star State"); **2.** roof became pointed; **3.** window widened; **4.** post removed.

■ **Military (Park) Maneuver,** *(page 31)* **1.** White stone turned gray; **2.** sword missing—employed in battle?; **3.** emblem upside down; **4.** statue base taller; **5.** circle moved right.

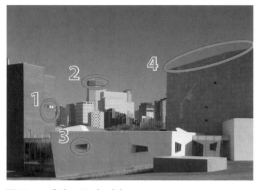

■ **Pioneer Square Search,** *(page 32)* **1.** Light fixtures removed; **2.** branches grew over building; **3.** windows joined; **4.** chimney moved right; **5.** light fixtures added.

■ **An Off Note,** *(page 33)* **1.** Bar segment missing in photo 2.

■ **Eye of the Beholder,** *(page 35)* **1.** Windows slid down; **2.** gray rooftop painted blue; **3.** opening changed shape; **4.** building grew taller.

■ **The Secret Garden,** *(page 36)* **1.** Flag taken down; **2.** more flowers planted; **3.** stone plaque raised; **4.** more yellow flowers bloomed; **5.** window bricked in.

■ **Old Faithful Finder,** *(page 34)* **1.** Hat added; **2.** strap switched shoulders; **3.** pink shirt became red; **4.** clouds swept away.

■ **Presidential Puzzler,** *(page 37)* **1.** Flag is to left of pole in picture 5.

■ **Puzzle Mountain Majesties,** *(page 38)*
1. Tree fell; **2.** mountain taller; **3.** tree lost its top;
4. tree grew.

■ **Dunes Day,** *(page 42)* **1.** Purple blossoms added;
2. blossoms removed; **3.** flower appeared; **4.** limb
longer; **5.** branch deleted.

■ **Cape May Cruise,** *(page 39)* **1.** Pole turned
black; **2.** bottom half of window missing; **3.** dormer
removed; **4.** plant and shadow deleted.

■ **Chichen Itza Chase,** *(page 43)* **1.** Edge filled in;
2. cloud drifted left; **3.** white shorts turned black;
4. person climbed steps; **5.** tourist added.

■ **A Visual
Narrative,**
(pages 44–45)
1. Corner tilted
up; **2.** red circle
added; **3.** white of
eye blackened;
4. arm bigger;
5. brown section
turned white.

■ **A Puzzle Divided,** *(pages 40–41)* **1.** Column
removed; **2.** person went home; **3.** rooftop deck added
(better view of the Mall); **4.** light pole shortened.

LEVEL 2

■ **A Lakeside Property,** *(page 46)* **1.** Mountain grew; **2.** tide covered the rocks; **3.** shoreline extended; **4.** clump of grass added; **5.** rock formation eroded; **6.** island added, **7.** grass deleted

■ *Peak***aboo,** *(page 47)* **1.** Rock removed; **2.** more grass in stream; **3.** snow melted; **4.** tree reflection added; **5.** mountaintop smoothed out; **6.** treetop removed.

■ **Launchpad Puzzle,** *(page 48)* **1.** Bird flew away; **2.** white orb enlarged; **3.** scaffolding lowered; **4.** ball added; **5.** black strip turned white; **6.** pole added.

■ **Heavenly Aspirations,** *(page 49)* **1.** Street lamp removed in picture 1.

■ **Portland Head Light Caper,** *(pages 50–51)* **1.** Roofline raised; **2.** stone removed; **3.** window boarded up; **4.** window added; **5.** brown rocks extended; **6.** sea calmed—foam gone; **7.** plant added.

■ **St. Paul's Cathedral Chase,** *(page 52)* **1.** Spire taller; **2.** column removed; **3.** stripe erased; **4.** window filled in; **5.** spire demolished; **6.** triangular top now arched.

175

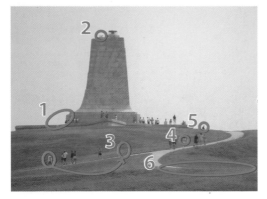

Flight of Fancy, *(page 53)* **1.** Side of base angled; **2.** rooftop structure missing; **3.** person moved up the path; **4.** blue shirt changed to pink; **5.** person went home; **6.** path extended.

Hidden Lake Hunt, *(page 54)* **1.** Stump enlarged; **2.** tip of outcropping gone; **3.** mountaintop removed; **4.** snow melted; **5.** stones enlarged; **6.** snow patch added.

The King's Castle, *(page 55)* **1.** Window panes removed; **2.** red flowers turned green; **3.** black oval enlarged; **4.** white line turned black; **5.** chimney moved right; **6.** arch turned upside down and moved up.

Volcanic Activity, *(page 56)* **1.** Brown shirt turned white in picture 3.

Lincoln's Cabin, *(page 57)* **1.** Trim missing; **2.** floor vent moved; **3.** darker strip lightened; **4.** ceiling detail removed; **5.** post top bigger; **6.** window added; **7.** post missing.

Bridge Over Troubled Waters, *(pages 58–59)* **1.** Post removed; **2.** leaves added; **3.** moss and plants gone—stone rolled?; **4.** water stream widened; **5.** rock added; **6.** branch pruned.

■ **Red Rock Riddler,** *(page 60)* **1.** Rock formation added; **2.** flower plucked; **3.** plants removed; **4.** flower added; **5.** mountaintop flattened; **6.** flower blossomed—yellow center now visible.

■ **Falls Finder,** *(page 63)* **1.** Fall's coming—red leaves added in picture 1.

■ **Pilgrims' Passage,** *(page 61)* **1.** Emblem upside down; **2.** two dark lines added; **3.** crow's nest extended; **4.** rope brace added; **5.** tide line lowered; **6.** brown section turned white; **7.** brown knob added.

■ **Brooklyn Bridge Bungle,** *(page 64)* **1.** Clouds added; **2.** building taller; **3.** pylons added; **4.** flag removed—blew away?; **5.** cable added; **6.** building top demolished; **7.** arch filled in.

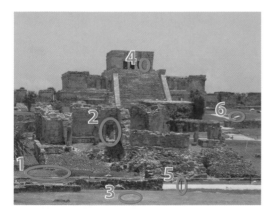

■ **Mayan Mystery,** *(page 62)* **1.** Grass grew over; **2.** doorway filled in; **3.** rock added; **4.** doorway added; **5.** black pole turned white; **6.** stone removed.

■ **Silversword Search,** *(page 65)* **1.** Mountain grew; **2.** rock added; **3.** silver tip turned green; **4.** plant added; **5.** plants removed; **6.** dark center brightened.

■ Pueblo Palace Puzzler, *(pages 66–67)*
1. Window bricked over; **2.** ladder added—easier access; **3.** window widened; **4.** wall collapsed; **5.** window added; **6.** ladder removed; **7.** path added.

■ Badlands Business, *(page 70)* **1.** Island in river deleted in picture 4.

■ *Bean* There, Done That, *(page 68)* **1.** Building taller; **2.** shadow extended—later in the day?; **3.** antenna added; **4.** person left; **5.** building reflection missing; **6.** windows removed.

■ Ghost Town Guesser, *(page 71)* **1.** Angled roof removed; **2.** hitching post missing; **3.** new banner put up ; **4.** beam added; **5.** BEATTY became BEAUTY; **6.** bench top turned dark brown; **7.** door latch lowered.

■ Vineyard Tour, *(page 69)* **1.** Trees cut down; **2.** vines grew over window; **3.** green sign added; **4.** dark brown shape removed; **5.** window moved right—better view; **6.** pipe moved down; **7.** post extended.

■ San Simeon Search, *(page 72)* **1.** Pillar removed; **2.** black line erased; **3.** statue added; **4.** globe disappeared; **5.** stone line removed; **6.** post and chain turned black.

■ **Waikiki Wander,** *(page 73)* **1.** Black roof turned white; **2.** people left the beach—too much sun; **3.** building grew taller; **4.** beach expanded; **5.** dark cloud shortened; **6.** white wave gone; **7.** building added.

■ **Two If by Sea,** *(page 77)* **1.** WELCOME TO removed from sign; **2.** another skylight added; **3.** post added; **4.** lighthouse stripes changed direction; **5.** white square removed; **6.** branches trimmed; **7.** sign upside down.

■ **A Devil of a Puzzle,** *(pages 74–75)* **1.** Fence now closed; **2.** screen became rectangular; **3.** chain removed; **4.** Devil's Tower shortened; **5.** white hatch removed; **6.** orange light turned red; **7.** white hose turned red.

■ **Historic Renovation,** *(pages 78–79)* **1.** Window shade drawn; **2.** bushes extended left; **3.** rooftop stacks added; **4.** leaf added; **5.** branches trimmed; **6.** cross became circle; **7.** white stone became brown.

■ **Hoodoo Hunt,** *(page 76)* **1.** Stone gap filled in; **2.** cloud added; **3.** rock rolled away; **4.** new tree sprouted; **5.** bush appeared; **6.** tree cut down.

■ **Set in Stone,** *(page 80)* **1.** Leaves fell; **2.** carving shrunk; **3.** star on wheel expanded; **4.** gold stripe added; **5.** number 60 changed to 90; **6.** emblem removed.

Beachfront Property, *(page 84)* **1.** Fence taller; **2.** shrub vanished; **3.** umbrellas switched; **4.** cloud blew away; **5.** chair missing; **6.** more furniture added.

View Variations, *(page 81)* **1.** Extra dome tower added; **2.** white dome made taller; **3.** tower disappeared; **4.** archway expanded for better access; **5.** black line missing; **6.** gold building demolished.

Grand Canyon Game, *(page 82)* **1.** Tree branch added in picture 2.

Teton Teaser, *(page 85)* **1.** Snow melted; **2.** tree added; **3.** branch trimmed; **4.** branch extended; **5.** plants covered rock; **6.** clouds drifted away.

Hilton Head Harbor, *(page 83)* **1.** Pole reflection extended; **2.** windows joined; **3.** green roof turned white; **4.** circular window added; **5.** red reflection turned white; **6.** white section turned black; **7.** person left.

On the Road Again, *(page 86)* **1.** Peak taller; **2.** grass added; **3.** broken center white line added; **4.** road widened; **5.** blue stripe extended; **6.** ladder missing; **7.** tree trunk removed.

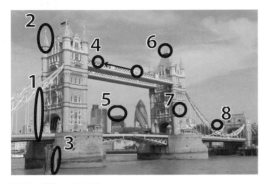

■ **Baffling Bridge,** *(page 87)* **1.** Cable clipped; **2.** turret taken down; **3.** pylon added; **4.** crown emblem moved left; **5.** building taller; **6.** gold ornament blew off; **7.** windows filled in; **8.** trees grew.

■ **Church Search,** *(pages 88–89)* **1.** Cloud grew; **2.** more white flowers appeared; **3.** column of windows filled in; **4.** person moved down and right; **5.** round window filled in; **6.** column missing; **7.** brown panel bigger; **8.** post added to fence.

■ **Museum Mix-up,** *(page 90)* **1.** Window boarded up; **2.** umbrella turned brown; **3.** column became solid gold; **4.** shape above window filled in; **5.** light fixture added; **6.** clouds appeared; **7.** shadow lowered—sun setting?; **8.** another chair appeared.

■ **Storied Estate,** *(page 91)* **1.** Branch pruned; **2.** white flowers plucked; **3.** window filled in; **4.** leaves appeared; **5.** reflection of window erased; **6.** cluster of leaves deleted; **7.** plants appeared; **8.** reflection of chimney vanished; **9.** dirt pathway widened.

■ **Back to Nature,** *(page 92)* **1.** Rock sank underwater in picture 5.

■ **Be on Your Guard,** *(page 93)* **1.** Horizontal bar added; **2.** wreath relief deleted; **3.** hands holding camera moved right; **4.** lantern fell off; **5.** heads switched places; **6.** gold knob removed; **7.** vertical bar erased; **8.** jacket turned blue; **9.** window bricked over.

Picturesque Park, *(page 94)* **1.** Ridge grew; **2.** trunk got thicker; **3.** tree turned green; **4.** car drove off; **5.** stop sign moved left; **6.** rock outcropping erased; **7.** ridge taller; **8.** GARDEN OF THE GODS erased; **9.** yellow line disappeared.

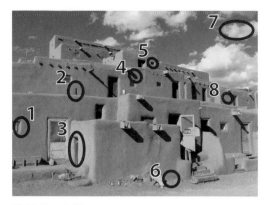

Valley Village, *(page 98)* **1.** Window moved up; **2.** chimney got taller; **3.** door filled in; **4.** shadow vanished; **5.** window filled in; **6.** rock appeared; **7.** cloud floated away; **8.** window added.

Out of the Blue, *(page 95)* **1.** Tree grew; **2.** section of building missing; **3.** red reflection longer; **4.** column appeared; **5.** lamppost added; **6.** building deleted; **7.** light's reflection erased; **8.** building taller.

Lifeguard on Duty, *(page 99)* **1.** Swim trunks turned blue; **2.** railing all green; **3.** post painted black; **4.** CLEAN deleted; **5.** flower disappeared; **6.** flower turned red; **7.** green flag bigger; **8.** umbrella now blue.

Parisian Puzzle, *(pages 96–97)* **1.** Trees added; **2.** bus turned red; **3.** person moved up and right; **4.** shirt turned green; **5.** antenna taller; **6.** star erased; **7.** person disappeared; **8.** building vanished.

Executive Privilege, *(page 100)* **1.** Bench deleted; **2.** window boarded up; **3.** chimney moved right; **4.** archway filled in; **5.** bench added; **6.** flowers became white; **7.** shrub grew taller; **8.** window gone; **9.** grass replaced flowerbed.

■ **Imperial Estate,** *(pages 104–105)* **1.** Fence posts taken down; **2.** hole in railing filled in; **3.** area became solid red; **4.** column appeared; **5.** ornament removed; **6.** column painted black; **7.** shadows moved; **8.** top of post fell off.

■ **Go with the Flow,** *(page 101)* **1.** Leaves fell from tree in picture 1.

■ **Life's a Beach,** *(page 102)* **1.** Skylight removed; **2.** person moved right; **3.** window added; **4.** cloud appeared; **5.** umbrellas switched colors; **6.** person swam out to sea; **7.** white square painted gray; **8.** column of windows erased.

■ **Transformed Terrace,** *(page 106)* **1.** Blossom plucked; **2.** person moved up and left; **3.** top of post missing; **4.** another flower bloomed; **5.** banner bigger; **6.** person ran off; **7.** backpack turned blue; **8.** second railing added.

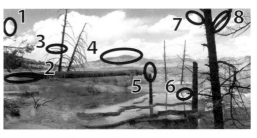

■ **Mammoth Search,** *(page 107)* **1.** Cloud drifted away; **2.** shadow extended left; **3.** limb fell; **4.** mountain taller; **5.** trunk taller; **6.** branch extended; **7.** branch appeared; **8.** branch snapped off.

■ **Beguiling Isle,** *(page 103)* **1.** Yellow flowers grew; **2.** flag and pole vanished; **3.** chair appeared; **4.** window added; **5.** tree grew; **6.** chimney added; **7.** flagpole longer; **8.** grass extended into road.

■ **Louisiana Landmark,** *(page 108)* **1.** Round window filled in picture 2.

■ **Tropical Paradise,** *(page 109)* **1.** Palm leaves blew off; **2.** blue chair appeared; **3.** raft turned pink; **4.** swimmer floated right; **5.** palm tree missing; **6.** palm leaf appeared; **7.** water line raised; **8.** chair turned pink.

■ **Riverside City,** *(pages 110–111)* **1.** Trees added; **2.** post vanished; **3.** boat appeared; **4.** building got shorter; **5.** cloud moved down and right; **6.** shadow of bridge disappeared; **7.** rectangular panel turned yellow; **8.** building appeared.

■ **The Birds,** *(page 112)* **1.** Bird's right wing extended—will it fly in circles now?; **2.** tower taller; **3.** someone decided to walk on wall; **4.** white shirt now black; **5.** arch squared off; **6.** person moved to left; **7.** bird flew away; **8.** new bird joined flock.

■ **Wild Wonderland,** *(page 113)* **1.** Windows covered over in picture 2.

■ **Changes in Chinatown,** *(page 114)* **1.** Horizontal strips extended across window; **2.** frame painted red; **3.** dragon lost horns; **4.** railing pattern changed; **5.** window bricked over; **6.** lantern tassels removed; **7.** lantern missing; **8.** light lowered; **9.** red lantern became yellow; **10.** waves washed away.

■ **Can't See the Forest for the Trees,** *(page 118)* **1.** Tree added in picture 1.

■ **Compare the Canals,** *(page 115)* **1.** Path covered with bushes; **2.** horizontal bar removed; **3.** rowboat painted white; **4.** trees added; **5.** palm tree appeared; **6.** canoe floated away; **7.** buildings disappeared; **8.** cement post appeared.

■ *Pier* **Review,** *(page 116)* **1.** Girder lines gone; **2.** flags switched positions; **3.** white border on boat now blue; **4.** letter V began to wonder Y; **5.** seats missing; **6.** buoys gone; **7.** lightpole taller; **8.** sign letters vanished; **9.** blue banners turned red; **10.** windows on boat boarded up.

■ **Altered Amphitheatre,** *(page 119)* **1.** Ridge appeared; **2.** grass grew; **3.** wall taller; **4.** cement block added; **5.** sign moved down and right; **6.** sign turned black; **7.** base turned blue; **8.** boulder added.

■ **Machu Picchu Quest,** *(page 120)* **1.** Alpaca moved up one level in picture 2.

■ **Hilltop Hunt,** *(page 117)* **1.** Tower moved left; **2.** dome tower taller; **3.** windows bricked over; **4.** tree replanted; **5.** window added; **6.** house completely overgrown with trees; **7.** window gone; **8.** new tree sprouted.

■ **Downtown Differences,** *(pages 124–125)* **1.** Building taller; **2.** pole shorter; **3.** window taller; **4.** fence post disappeared; **5.** signs (in shadow) switched places; **6.** stripe missing; **7.** turret turned white; **8.** white stripe added; **9.** window shade pulled down.

■ **Water Under the Bridge,** *(page 121)*
1. Silhouette vanished; **2.** support pillar covered in shadow; **3.** red flag turned blue; **4.** swan appeared; **5.** spire removed; **6.** support pillar sunk; **7.** hill taller; **8.** wooden wall extended to water line; **9.** window added.

■ **City Cluster,** *(page 126)* **1.** Satellite dish grew; **2.** tri-level chimney leveled; **3.** chimney removed; **4.** window bricked in; **5.** spire shape changed; **6.** white bar removed; **7.** rooftop decoration taller—the better to impress the neighbors!

■ **Suspend Your Disbelief,** *(page 122)*
1. Building extended left; **2.** flag switched direction; **3.** building altered; **4.** column taller; **5.** off-white bricks turned brown; **6.** flag removed; **7.** shadow appeared; **8.** roof painted black.

■ **Ellis Island Inspection,** *(page 127)* **1.** Hill appeared; **2.** flag and pole moved left; **3.** grass paved over; **4.** roof turned black; **5.** flag vanished; **6.** window bricked over; **7.** top of tower disappeared; **8.** new grass planted.

■ **Red Square Search,** *(page 123)* **1.** Section of building turned brown; **2.** people switched places; **3.** lights added; **4.** blue stripe became white; **5.** square turned green; **6.** white stripe deleted; **7.** cross erased; **8.** spire turned orange; **9.** spire deleted.

LEVEL 4

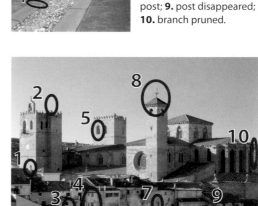

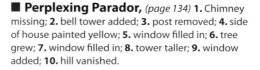

■ **Modified Mill,** *(page 128)* **1.** Hill extended; **2.** tunnel filled with shadow; **3.** branches trimmed; **4.** tree bigger; **5.** window added; **6.** tree added; **7.** reflection vanished; **8.** roof taller; **9.** spoke in waterwheel erased; **10.** trunk of tree uprooted.

■ **Monumental Challenge,** *(page 129)* **1.** Ridge higher in picture 6.

■ **Seattle Search,** *(page 130)* **1.** Cloud blew away; **2.** building taller; **3.** building became solid white; **4.** building appeared; **5.** plant grew; **6.** spaces in base filled in; **7.** skyscraper taller; **8.** building missing; **9.** building disappeared; **10.** building turned blue.

■ **Altered Alcatraz,** *(page 131)* **1.** Trees cut down; **2.** smokestack appeared; **3.** top of tower turned brown; **4.** crossbeams removed; **5.** hill taller; **6.** windows filled in; **7.** lighthouse taller; **8.** row of windows bricked in; **9.** small building deleted; **10.** building escaped.

■ **Alley Overhaul,** *(pages 132–133)* **1.** Groove in sidewalk filled in; **2.** hinge missing; **3.** shutter erased; **4.** shutter turned red; **5.** red post painted black; **6.** window bricked over; **7.** cloud appeared; **8.** black ring added to post; **9.** post disappeared; **10.** branch pruned.

■ **Perplexing Parador,** *(page 134)* **1.** Chimney missing; **2.** bell tower added; **3.** post removed; **4.** side of house painted yellow; **5.** window filled in; **6.** tree grew; **7.** window filled in; **8.** tower taller; **9.** window added; **10.** hill vanished.

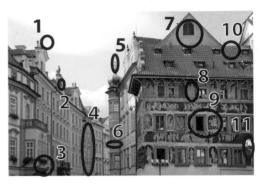

■ See Versailles, *(page 135)* **1.** Yellow flowers planted; **2.** border connected; **3.** tree appeared; **4.** gargoyle on the loose—it's gone!; **5.** window filled in; **6.** white blossoms plucked; **7.** woman moved left; **8.** small building turned yellow; **9.** window bricked up; **10.** border vanished.

■ Classic Architecture Puzzle, *(page 138)* **1.** Statue added on rooftop; **2.** circle vanished; **3.** window plant larger; **4.** red border filled in; **5.** spire taller; **6.** yellow rectangles now blue; **7.** window larger; **8.** window added; **9.** panels switched; **10.** extra window built; **11.** lights added.

■ Cavernous Challenge, *(page 136)* **1.** Shadow got bigger in picture 3.

■ Boothbay Harbor Hunt, *(page 139)* **1.** Boat slip extended; **2.** boat motored in; **3.** pier removed; **4.** ship sinking; **5.** blue roof turned red; **6.** white tower painted black; **7.** boat larger; **8.** tree cut down; **9.** cars drove home; **10.** pier moved to right side of bridge.

■ On the Waterfront, *(page 137)* **1.** Yellow house became green; **2.** laundry appeared; **3.** blue rectangles on boat turned green; **4.** pole shadows missing; **5.** mailbox removed from white door; **6.** light removed; **7.** bushes disappeared; **8.** white window frames turned red; **9.** antenna taken down; **10.** laundry missing; **11.** extra chimney sprouted; **12.** boat floated away.

■ Full Steam Ahead, *(pages 140–141)* **1.** Leaves appeared; **2.** grass grew; **3.** smoke blew off; **4.** number 3 changed direction; **5.** numbers 7 and 8 switched places; **6.** chain longer; **7.** sign removed; **8.** trestle missing; **9.** leaves appeared; **10.** another trestle appeared.

■ **Harpers Ferry Feat,** *(page 142)* **1.** Door filled in; **2.** chain gone—how does that sign stay up?; **3.** post on bench missing; **4.** handle moved up; **5.** ridge raised; **6.** dormer deleted; **7.** window added; **8.** sign moved left; **9.** shutter deleted; **10.** door pane covered.

■ **New York, New York,** *(page 145)* **1.** Poles added to roller coaster; **2.** building became taller; **3.** window turned white; **4.** building grew—envious of other buildings; **5.** window filled in; **6.** skyscraper left—couldn't take the pressure; **7.** words erased; **8.** side of building became solid orange; **9.** awning turned red; **10.** palm tree appeared.

■ **Temple Square Search,** *(pages 146–147)* **1.** Trees grew; **2.** gap in trees filled in; **3.** spire taller; **4.** round window became square; **5.** two cement lines added; **6.** new window; **7.** roof turned black; **8.** shadow bigger; **9.** roof of building darker.

■ **Meet Me in St. Louis,** *(page 143)* **1.** Train went to station; **2.** steeple moved right; **3.** building turned black; **4.** building taller; **5.** tree grew; **6.** building disappeared; **7.** ST. LOUIS erased; **8.** tree cut down; **9.** grass added; **10.** horizon line raised.

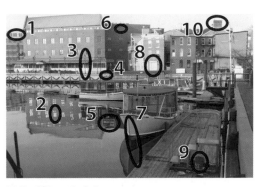

■ **Mystery in Mystic,** *(page 144)* **1.** Seagull did an about-face in picture 5.

■ **Baffling Baltimore,** *(page 148)* **1.** White section of building turned brown; **2.** reflection of window missing; **3.** lamppost taken down; **4.** WATER disappeared; **5.** reflection of sign vanished; **6.** window appeared; **7.** blue rope added; **8.** window frame became black; **9.** bucket turned blue; **10.** chimney taller.

■ Castle on the Bluff, *(page 149)* **1.** Trees cut down; **2.** car drove off; **3.** roof turned brown; **4.** spire taller; **5.** car turned red; **6.** window filled in; **7.** tower missing; **8.** antenna taller; **9.** brick filled gap in ledge; **10.** roof became gray.

■ King of the Castle, *(page 152)* **1.** Window moved up; **2.** shrub grew; **3.** careful!—railing missing; **4.** shadow disappeared; **5.** hole filled in; **6.** flowerpot appeared; **7.** red part of flag turned green; **8.** jet of water erased; **9.** window filled in; **10.** splash from fountain larger.

■ Hoover Dam Dilemma, *(page 150)* **1.** Shadow of vehicle and trailer vanished; **2.** ridge missing; **3.** bushes grew; **4.** cylindrical tower turned black; **5.** minivan drove away; **6.** tower disappeared; **7.** van turned red; **8.** car moved down and right; **9.** tower added; **10.** grass grew.

■ Building an Empire, *(page 153)* **1.** Window filled in; **2.** palm leaf deleted; **3.** palm leaf turned yellow; **4.** roof detail removed; **5.** branch erased; **6.** white rectangle disappeared; **7.** spokes turned black; **8.** rectangle larger; **9.** black rope added; **10.** lantern deleted.

■ Survey the Sandstone..., *(pages 154–155)* **1.** Bush grew; **2.** rock bigger—rocks can grow?; **3.** people moved on; **4.** patch of sky covered with rock; **5.** person left; **6.** shrub deleted; **7.** shrub appeared; **8.** rocks erased; **9.** shrub added; **10.** shrub larger.

■ Ivy League Exam, *(page 151)* **1.** Top section of roof missing; **2.** boulder bigger; **3.** gap in trees filled in; **4.** archway added; **5.** windows filled in; **6.** section of roof turned orange; **7.** horizontal stripe appeared; **8.** people moved right; **9.** boulder appeared; **10.** tower taken down.

■ **Something's Fishy,** *(page 156)* **1.** Row of windows filled in; **2.** dock and boat vanished; **3.** roof turned black; **4.** rowboat moved left; **5.** window widened—for a better view; **6.** house painted tan; **7.** tree grew; **8.** window appeared; **9.** flagpole taken down; **10.** house turned yellow.

■ **Fountain Frenzy,** *(page 157)* **1.** Jet of water appeared; **2.** splash settled; **3.** splash larger; **4.** base of statue taller; **5.** tree cut down; **6.** statue changed direction; **7.** striped flag taken down; **8.** statue disappeared; **9.** stream of water stopped; **10.** grass extended on ledge.

■ **A Graceful Entry,** *(page 158)* **1.** Orange flowers changed to yellow; **2.** crossbar added; **3.** stone urn appeared; **4.** base of cow statue missing; **5.** car drove off; **6.** carving removed from top of column; **7.** blue base painted gray; **8.** globe removed from light fixture; **9.** light fixture added; **10.** sidewalk missing; **11.** window top missing; **12.** circular window filled in.

■ ***Inn*dulge in a Challenge,** *(page 159)* **1.** Umbrella blew away; **2.** armrest fell off; **3.** umbrella pole missing; **4.** chimney taller; **5.** board grew; **6.** chimney missing; **7.** window filled in; **8.** roof taller; **9.** tree sprouted; **10.** flag expanded.

■ **Building Colors,** *(page 160)* **1.** Cord removed; **2.** lamp holder missing; **3.** green slat added; **4.** window boarded up; **5.** window lowered; **6.** sun turned black—is there an eclipse?; **7.** window taller; **8.** red slat removed; **9.** window added; **10.** X added.

■ **Panoramic Puzzle,** *(page 161)* **1.** Building deleted; **2.** top of tower removed; **3.** buildings taller; **4.** clouds extended; **5.** part of spire erased; **6.** tree grew taller; **7.** window appeared; **8.** window bricked over; **9.** window filled in; **10.** black tile removed; **11.** white tile turned black; **12.** tile became completely yellow.

■ **On the Boardwalk,** *(page 162)* **1.** Another bird flew in; **2.** light is on; **3.** building story turned black; **4.** restaraunt sign moved down; **5.** telephone sign removed; **6.** TAJ MAHAL became MAHAL TAJ; **7.** windows filled in; **8.** black roof turned white; **9.** extra tent set up; **10.** building taller; **11.** tent turned blue.

■ **Contend with the Canal,** *(page 166)* **1.** Top of building enlarged; **2.** tree grew; **3.** curtains closed for privacy; **4.** molding crumbled off; **5.** window bricked over; **6.** black boat bumper turned white; **7.** red stripes became white; **8.** window added to van; **9.** blue sign removed; **10.** oval window became square.

■ **Devilish Duty,** *(page 163)* **1.** Divot with plant filled in picture 1.

■ **Wondrous Wall,** *(page 167)* **1.** Tower vanished in picture 2.

■ **State-of-the-Art Building,** *(pages 164–165)* **1.** Windows filled in; **2.** building taller; **3.** white sections of antenna became black; **4.** three windows became one; **5.** building shy—hid behind other building; **6.** lightning rod removed; **7.** windows on roof filled in; **8.** UNION SQUARE erased; **9.** column of windows added; **10.** cloud disappeared.

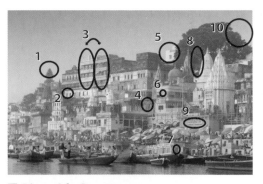

■ **Riverside Secrets,** *(page 168)* **1.** Roof bigger; **2.** windows bricked in; **3.** facades switched; **4.** tree planted; **5.** building vanished; **6.** window shade turned orange; **7.** window gone; **8.** spire added; **9.** sign removed; **10.** trees filled in skyline.